WELCOME HOME
Vietnam

WELCOME HOME
Vietnam

BY COL. CHUCK SANDERS

Strategic Book Group
Durham, Connecticut

Strategic Book Group
P. O. Box 333
Durham, CT 06422
http://www.strategicbookclub.com

ISBN: 978-1-60976-242-1

Book Design by Julius Kiskis

Printed in the United States of America
18 17 16 15 14 13 12 11 10   1 2 3 4 5

Dedication

This book is dedicated to those spouses, children and loved ones of the Vietnam combat veteran for enduring the stress and pain of loving us that suffer Post Traumatic Stress Disorder.

I would like to express my sincerest appreciation for my brother Jon (Bonsai) Morishita who sat with me as I shed tears of pain and loss never being judgmental and always showing that love and respect only two brothers and warriors can know.

Lastly and most significant I want to express my Love, Respect and Appreciation for the woman who chose to spend her life with me and in so doing deals with my nightmares, sleepless nights, anxiety attacks, panic attacks and occasional paranoia. Behind every good man is a great woman! Thank you! Maraia C.E. Sanders for your Love, Dedication, Faith and Forgiveness. Many Thanks goes to our son Troy G.R.E. Sanders for never giving up on me when I had on many occasions wanted to give up and crawl in a bottle or just put an end to the pain and suffering my mind would not let me forget.

Contents

Contents

The Cover Of The Book And The Man Who Drew It!

he cover of the book depicts a soldier being wounded in combat. The Grim Reaper has pounced upon him and as he lay dying the Corpsman/medic arrives on the scene to fix his wounds before he dies of the them, bleeds to death or gets an infection, one of the rare times when man was able to defeat the Grim Reaper and rob death of its victim. The grim reaper has turned away as the soldier is saved and will survive the wounds now. If you notice the trees have faces, they were calling out to the Angel of Death! Death lurks from every tree and rock. It was not his time, not today, not at this moment in the cycle of life.

The drawing is by a dear friend we will call Charlie Brown a Vietnamese/American (referred to as Amerasian or Namer's by Americans). Charlie Brown was born in Danang Vietnam in 1954, the son of an American in Vietnam for a specific mission, to bring in guns and tanks and ammunition as per an agreement with the South Vietnamese Government and the American Central Intelligence Agency in response to an agreement with the President of the United States and the South Vietnamese President, the French were losing the war and pulling out. His mother was a South Vietnamese Nurse. To the general population in America we were not in Vietnam at this time and most of us civilians had still

1

not heard of Vietnam, Laos, Cambodia or Thailand yet. They were still referred to and taught in the schoolbooks as Southeast Asia.

Charlie Brown was given to a rich South Vietnamese Family when he was very young. His Father had been reassigned to a stateside post. His mother could not take care of him as a single parent and working full time as a nurse. Not to mention it would have been a disgrace to have a child out of wedlock at that point in time, especially a half breed American and Vietnamese. The family raised Charlie Brown until he was ten and then everything changed. The family was now in fear for their life as the communists were killing Vietnamese people with the Amerasian children. It was considered a disgrace to the race so they were forced to put the ten year old in the streets as though they had never heard of him and they left him to fend for himself. It may sound horrific to some, but people will do strange things when their lives are on the line and especially since he was not theirs in the first place so they were not about to jeopardize their lives and their Vietnamese children's lives for him.

In the streets of Danang he did not know where his next meal would come from or where he would lay his head for sleep safely. Along come the Marines and they found him wandering aimlessly around so they brought him back to the Camp with them where they learned he was homeless and they took him in and fed him and made him one of their own. They gave him his name Charlie Brown after the famous cartoon character, which he carries to date.

Charlie Brown became a Marine at the age of ten, he went on patrols with the Marines, learned how to speak English by the Marines, you can imagine some of his vocabulary was rather rich with profanity. By the time he was twelve, which would have been 1966 he was working as an interpreter, he was taught how to fire the M-14 rifle, M-60 Machine gun, the Rifle Propelled Grenade Launcher, M-79 and most everything else in our arsenal of small arms. He was a gifted child, he learned quickly. He was taught how to operate the radio and as time went he watched and learned how to call in air strikes, medical evacuations and even artillery. His ability to read maps and the compass was unsurpassed by most any of the regular ground pounders. He was also taught to read from comic books, Playboy magazines and the likes, the type magazines and books one would expect to be around a Marine compound. He had a gift for drawing and he was given pencils and drawing pads. He probably drew every Marine in his particular units girlfriend and wife. As time passed he was actually given a rank by the local Marine Commander. By age 15 he was a Private First Class and authorized to go to the Post Exchange to purchase cleaning gear, candies and whatever else he wanted. He went to the barbershop and wore his hair like Marines. Each payday the Marines would take a collection and place it in a box for Charlie Brown's pay. The Marines are a funny bred, if they like you they will go out of their way to do you right and Charlie Brown was liked very much. He had become a viable asset to the Marines. After the collection was taken Charlie Brown was doing very well in the pay category. He lived with the Marines until 1971 when the Marines for all intensive purposes had started their reduction in force in Vietnam, which meant they were pulling out. He was now seventeen and one of the best Combat Marines on the compound if not the best trained.

At this point Charlie Brown left the Marines with a strong recommendation from everyone from the Commander down to the lowliest Private. He went to live with the Army Special Forces and was taught how to parachute and repel out of Helicopters and down steep hills, along with many other survival techniques. Again he proved himself a tremendous asset to the Army and our mission. He stayed with the Army Special Forces until they pulled out in 1975 with the fall of Saigon in April of that year. He was all alone and had no idea where he was going to go so he used his expert training and avoided the Khmer Rough, the North Vietnamese and the Viet Cong for four long years hiding in the woods and fighting them. Finally after four years in 1979 he was captured and sent to a reeducation camp for reprogramming. The only reason he was not killed on the spot was because his reputation preceded him the Communists felt when they reeducated him he would be a good example to all the other Amerasians and all those others who worked with or for the Americans. After two years he escaped, he was gone for another four years which would be 1985, he was recaptured and both his legs were broke so he could not run and they put the fear of the communist forces in him so he would denounce the Americans as criminals and accept the communist doctrine. He played their deadly game until he healed and then once again he was in the wind, escaped. He then gathered the Amerasians and became their protector and taught them to fight and protect themselves. We were now into 1987-1988 and America was meeting with the Vietnamese Communists to locate remains of our military when Charlie Brown was found and an agreement was made to bring him back to America.

He was taken to CIA headquarters in Up-State New York but it was way too cold for him and he could not handle it so he escaped and went to Hawaii. After they located him they allowed him to stay in Hawaii provided he underwent Psychiatric treatment on-going indefinitely. He lives on a meager income given to him by the government of five hundred a month and food stamps as well as medical care. He earned far more then we could ever repay him, and way more then they will ever give him. He is not bitter and is a loving caring man that is multitalented. He can outwork any two men and has developed a talent for doing tile work and a multitude of other viable talents. He lives alone and loves children, possibly because he never had a childhood of his own, he was a child warrior. He has a great appreciation for the Marine Vietnam veteran.

There were many left behind just like him, some never lived with the military, but were the product of American Military and Vietnamese women. Most were left behind and forced to fend for themselves not allowed to enter the public schools and live off handouts and what they can dig in the garbage for or steal to survive. They are treated worse then the dogs that run the streets and not allowed American status by the American Government. Many are diseased and psychologically impaired. Several just wither up and die from disease, infection or just give up living. Unknown to mainstream society in America and never acknowledged as human by the people and government of the new Vietnam. People without a country and merely surviving from one day to the next, for them the war will never end.

The Amerasians or Namer's are considered by our government as merely collateral damage and not even given a second thought, yet we call ourselves a Godly nation. We feed the hungry in Africa, protect the whales easily forgetting the damage, pain and suffering these people are forced to undergo daily.

When the Day Begins

Finally the sun starts to slowly creep up and the darkness turns to light. We made it through another night, one night closer to life, one day less of living dead.

We seek the path of least resistance but that has somehow caste us onto the road to or from hell. Have we somehow unknowingly been cast into hell and now only surviving to face another night of this living hell? Are we really living or is this someplace in between the living and dead? Will it actually end or have we been forever placed in this situation or world for all eternity, after all, reality and dream world have become one, nothing is real and nothing is false, It just is! Day again becomes night and if we are lucky we will again see night become day. The faces of those we know and have known become entangled caricatures and there voices merely cries or utterances without meaning, the living and dead have crossed the line and are now somehow bound and bonded together in some brutal but cohesive union. Pain is constant and becomes our friend, we lavish in it as it has become our lover and carries us to the psychological climax of orgasm knowing through it we are still alive. Alive to serve whatever cause we are somehow being led or misled to believe. Then we arrive here and reality sets in, it sets in hard and fast.

The only real cause is the cause that we are from a lower caste of the American hierarchy. The Working poor, we could not afford draft deferments. We are dedicated, we love our country, and our God, and our family, Loyalty, and I think that is the word, yes! That is it! We are loyal American citizens. We are merely paying the price for our freedom and the freedom of those that put us down, those that pass judgment on us, those that are enjoying the freedom we can only dream of. We should feel good knowing we are the sword of justice, the providers of freedom and justice, but are we really? With each firefight or ambush we survive, the question becomes more prevalent. Are we really the winners, we are the ones destined to live with our personal demons for eternity? Those that died in one of these firefights or ambushes are freed up, no more worry, the war is over along with all the horrors that go with it.

We survive another night to survive another day of this living death. Darkness brings out the evil that hides away during the day for fear of being picked out or noticed as the evil it truly is, evil itself thrives in the darkness! Just like the country song by Charlie Pride, The snakes crawl at night! Who have we become? Are we not just like them? Just like those we came to destroy, to defeat. What separates us from them? Initially it was ideology, now after the passage of time we are merely trying to survive, are we not? Mercenaries wearing a uniform, poorly paid, and looked down on by our own people. Our mission is reduced to merely surviving another night of the living demons, those soldiers who are walking dead but have not yet laid down and let the shadows of death encompass them and lead them to the other side if there is such a thing. If we die does it end or do we just take on different bodies and pick up another weapon and relive it all over again? Maybe Heaven is the ignorance of our youth and exists only for the innocent. For us we have crossed the line, is there ever truly a return or have we forever crossed the invisible line of right and wrong, that programming that has molded us from our infancy to the ways mainstream society dictates we should think or feel? Where or what is morality? Is morality a programmed thought process that is taught to us from our youth through the Jewish / Christian philosophy and differs from the rest of the world? We attempt to feed and fight wars for other countries and yet we allow our own people to starve and live in the streets. We have changed, us that experience the survival mode of life because of a war we were thrown into and our values and morality has been compromised as well. Are we so irreparably changed or broken that we have crossed through that code of mainstream societies dictates and now all is fair game? Rape, murder, theft, molestation, and any other action that allows us to accomplish our mission and bring self-gratification to us the elite, the group who holds the most firepower or learns to fight the best. Are we cursed to live aimlessly trying to get back to the other side of the line to be socially acceptable?

Perception, Perception I am told is everything, how we perceive things becomes our reality. Then is reality not based on what we have learned through our programming starting in our infancy? If we see evil, then evil rules, and if we see good, then does good rule? But how from what we see in the right here and now is real good or evil? Can we again become good or are we irreparably damaged, changed in ways that even we do not know or understand? What is the great design? Did it ever really exist or is like the Easter Bunny and Santa Claus, another lie we are taught from our youth. If it does actually exist then has it been altered by the winds of time? Have we become the instruments used to instrument change? Maybe we are the change! Maybe there had never been change and nothing was ever what it was professed to have been, it is all a form of virtual reality brought out and put into use whenever it is deemed necessary? How did it ever get to this point where what appeared to be one thing was something entirely different and never was what it was professed to have been. How did we ever get to this point of confusion? Are we just puppets controlled by some supreme beings? Are our so-called leaders being controlled by some supreme being that causes them to have us dance whatever jig they desire?

We actively seek the path of God when we should be seeking the face of God, we as Christians are told that in the Bible in Psalms 27:8, "My heart says of you, "Seek His face!" Your face, Lord, I will seek. Of course this coins the question of who is God? Where is God? Why does it appear he turns his head to certain cultures, peoples and societies? Is it just the luck of the draw that we are born in a country professing freedom instead of a communist ruled country? Are some lives less significant or are we all insignificant and bred as cannon fodder, expendables or replacement items. Why is it we have to violate the law of morality in order to establish human law? Well developed and thought out plans never leave more questions then answers. Are there answers to situations or only compromise that leads to more questions for us to seek answers to? We talk of objectivity but how can you be objective when the object is unclear or unknown. Just focus I hear, but what do we focus on and in what direction do I focus, and on what do we focus on?

For now I will fight until I die or die until I fight again.

Don't You Remember Me?

As I lay down to sleep last night I asked God to give me a vision, some insight on Heaven and Hell. What was the difference from a layman's viewpoint? I felt I was living in both worlds here on earth, and having a difficult time breaking through.

Somewhere during the night (I did not know if I was asleep or not) I was in that place somewhere between reality and the dream world. I was somehow transported to a place just outside a big iron gate that was elaborately decorated. Yet it seemed somehow tasteful and distasteful at the same time, a contradiction in every way. I looked around as if I were supposed to meet someone or something at this gate. The gate seemed quite out of the ordinary, there seemed to be no entryway, no latch or way to get in either through, over, under or around. There were pictures of the grim reaper on the gate, pictures of rainbows with the most elaborate colors, angels danced in the gate, faces distorted from pain and suffering, flowers and fires, jewels and crosses, some black without light and some light without darkness. Then a strange light appeared before me. It was bright but I could not take my eyes off it. I was somehow transported through, over, or around the gate; I really do not know which.

I was taken to a place I had never seen before, somehow

I knew, or felt, I had been there in another life or another time. There was this wood plank bridge, a 2X12, with a rapid flowing waterway under it. It lapped at the board that was the bridge and went over this waterway from one side to the other. I thought this strange that just a 2X12 board was the bridge since it was a good 50 yards to the other side. On one side was a well- groomed grassy area that was equal to the beauty of the best golf courses and on the side outside the gate was a gravelly road.

On the other side was a beautiful hotel, or at least it appeared to be a hotel, motel or something like that, being a common man I do not know the difference. I do know inside was a fabulous parlor or reception room with very common and plain forgettable assistants. They all looked the same and dressed in exactly the same outfits, some form of uniform or something, their hair was exactly the same and they all had the same semi-smile, not a frown and not a smile, somewhere in between. It was very hard to tell what was going on in this place, as there were so many people. They all seemed to be in a hurry but were going nowhere. Once you entered the building there were no doors or windows leading out of it. Inside were many rooms and in each of the rooms there were people I could somehow recognize. But I could not remember from where I had known them. Mostly they wore partial Marine Corps uniforms. There were a couple Army, a few sailors, but mostly Marines. As I was somehow driven down the halls to each room, I began to notice that with each partial uniformed person there was something missing. In the first room there was a Marine in dress blue trousers and a civilian shirt and his arm would be missing. Then in the next room was a young Marine with his leg missing, wearing jungle utility blouse, civilian shorts. The one that distressed me most was a person in a Navy uniform, dress blue blouse with no lower body, his entire lower body was missing yet he was somehow alive, or was he, was anyone here for that matter really alive?

These rooms with the people in them in partial uniforms seemed to continue on for an eternity. I felt like I had stepped off into a Stephen King story. There were people with eyes missing and ears gone, jaws rotted out, one with an iron lung with just the backside of a Marine dress blue uniform. There was a myriad of diseased and mutilated beings all in these partial uniforms. I found myself wanting to look away but I could not, my mind and heart would not allow me to, or was it the source that was leading me to and through this place or dream world place in this nightmarish dream, at least I think it was a dream. Maybe it was the force or Spirit that was leading me down the halls and into and out of the rooms. I did all I could to avoid the eyes but my head kept being jerked up. I was forced to see the creased jaws and faces with deep pits from the tears that had fallen for so long they had stained and forced creases in the faces. I could see the fear and pain that had been forever embossed upon their faces. As I continued down the halls and in and out of the rooms, I could hear my name being called. I could hear the question coming through " Don't you remember me?" " Don't you remember me?" " Where were you?" "Where were you?" What was even more strange was they were not actually talking to me as I entered the rooms and halls but like some subliminal message or something. It continued to get louder as I passed farther down the hall. As I got to the end, or what I thought was the end it was as if there was an intercom device in my head, screaming my name along with "Don't you remember me?" " Where were you?"

I felt I would truly lose my mind and I was on the very brink of insanity. The voices and faces were completely enveloping my every thought. I fell to the ground. I covered my head and balled up in the fetal position (In an effort to escape, hide, or whatever I thought I was doing) to stop the voices and faces. Had I somehow caused these injuries or turned away when I could have possibly helped? Was it all somehow my fault?

Somehow I was transported to another place and mysteriously pulled into an upright position to continue on this strange journey never getting any of these questions answered or even commented on.

The State of Incomplete

I found myself in a peaceful village (at least seemingly so). I took inventory of everything around me. I noticed nothing had been completed. There was a house or hut partially built, and farther down, a fence strung to nowhere. There were a few posts and some wire but many breaks in between as if it had been started and stopped and some places without wire or posts at all. There was a chicken coup with no chickens and no gate on it. How I knew it was suppose to be a chicken coup, I have not a clue. There was a garden, it was plowed but there was nothing planted. Some yards were cut and some were overgrown. Then it hit me, where were the people? I had not seen even one person, or even one living thing. There were not even birds, no sounds of crickets, or any other life source.

Was this my life? To be alone with no one around and nothing completed. Was this the sign of things to be? Just me with nothing in life finished and some things barely started. Where were the people? Where were the dogs, the cats, chickens or even rodents? Surely I was not expected to finish everything alone. I continued to look and there was no- one. No animals, people, or even a feeling that I was truly there. Where was this place, who was I suppose to meet or know here? What was the purpose for this place anyhow?

14

It seemed like I was standing there forever and got no response to my thought question, I could hear the thought I did not know where it came from. Just that it came from somewhere inside of me. Then it came to me. Seek answers in the Church. I found the Church House, and it appeared to be the only building fully intact. It appeared as though there was no one there. A voice or an utterance came to me to seek the answers in the East at the altar.

I traveled through this large temple and went to the altar for the answers. As I prayed, it appeared as though my eyes opened up and in front of me were all the parishioners. They were all dead; at least from my limited knowledge of where I was and what the true definition of life and death was they were in fact dead. I began to scream (at least I think I was screaming). My mouth was open and I was totally enveloped in fear. I do not know if it was my voice screaming or the voice of the Light guiding me. In a sad but loud voice it came to me I was the Shepard and the flock were my sheep. Because of my inability to complete anything they had all given up. Their spirits were taken while I was away and slept or too preoccupied in my own personal agenda items. I had failed to put on the full armor (as I was taught). Because of this the demons (possibly Satan himself) had slipped in and played havoc! Again as I was ready to completely go over the edge of no return, when this strange light somehow transported me to another area, but the memory was not erased, it was like a feeling of falling and just at the very second before you hit bottom and was completely crushed from the fall I was pulled up, it was still hard etched in my mind and heart, the state of incomplete.

I began to take note of my personal life, and everything I

had ventured in life was never completed, almost but never totally complete, I had lived a life of many incompletes and there was no way of going back to complete them, they were to be forever incomplete in my heart and mind. My career, my education, my marriages, my child rearing, and my goals and personal mission in this life all seemed incomplete at this time. Even the war in Vietnam was cut short before we completed what we had came here to do, and it was all out of my control. All the young lives lost for what? There would be no ticker tape parade for us, only the haunting memories of incompleteness, and the incomplete state of my entire life looking me in the face asking the question what would my next mission be that I would ultimately fail to complete. I had even failed to complete ending my own life; I screwed it up and took the wrong medications, was found and hospitalized where I slept for three days only to awaken back in this world of incomplete. How many more people and things would be irreparably damaged before I completed something. Just as I was ready to break down and cry myself in to oblivion, I was again transported to another place or time. The memory as with all the others would remain forever haunting me.

Pop Up Target

I again was forced to refocus. I found myself in a big field with elephant grass. The elephant grass was at least ten to twelve feet high and so thick I could not see a foot in front of me I was lost. I had no idea where I was, what time or date it was so there was no way of comparing a time in my life to the place I was at this moment. One thing I was absolutely sure of was this place was not the most hospitable or human friendly place I could have been taken to. It was definitely not a place I would have chosen to go to, and I could hear strange sounds. There were sounds of a tiger or some kind of big cat, with the sound of crickets and birds and several other things I could not place or define. There was a feeling of nervous anticipation. I had this funny feeling in the pit of my stomach kind of nauseating and exciting at the same time a feeling of impending doom or a sense of extreme urgency. There was an instant erection like a young boy would get when something exciting was happening or about to happen. The same feeling I got, as a kid when this special girl I really thought was a beauty, said she would go to the dance with me. I had to ask my childcare person to teach me to dance; at least enough to get by. Thank God for the belly rubbing dances of the early sixties. Where were all the people, if I was here, surely there were team members somewhere, but I did not see or hear them?

Then I heard a rustling in the grasses. It was as though someone or something was crawling up next to me. There was the vague sound of metal clicking against metal, the sound of a round being chambered in a rifle. This was a sound you would become adamantly aware of. I looked down and saw tracks, the type tracks made by Vietnamese wearing sandals crafted from discarded tires. As I stood and looked in front of me, I saw a Viet Cong soldier, young looking but weathered from fighting in the jungles and heavy grasses. He had a rifle, and it was pointing at me. I had my shotgun pointing at him. It seemed as though a life- time had passed before I pulled the trigger it was as though I was somehow waiting for him to pull the trigger and I would feel the piercing of the full metal jacket of the round as it entered my chest, I would feel the impact and it would literally knock me to the ground and I would replay everything one more time as my life source spilled into the ground in this foreign country void of all my loved ones and those I thought loved me. I had my doubts of what love was or if it really even existed.

In slow motion the round balls that spilled out of my shotgun known as buckshot made their way toward him. I could see the small round balls began to penetrate his flesh. Spurts of blood shot out from every entry hole. Then his complete backside literally exploded in front of me. It made the time we faced each other a lifetime; at least the remainder of life for him.

Maybe this was a good thing. The only life he would ever know here on this earth would be fighting and war. I knew as I trembled in fear and urinated all over myself that it could and almost did go the other way. The part that scared me the most was that I did not care. I quit caring whether I lived or died. This is when the reality hit home that this was the young me, the young me that somehow had died and continued to live in a body void of life. As rapidly as it had all happened (which of course to me seemed forever), I was transported to another place.

Operation Point Hill 200

I regained consciousness and, my bearings or whatever one would call it; I noticed I was on top of this hill. There were other people around, all in combat uniforms, Camouflage trousers, green tee shirts, flak jackets, and helmets. Everyone had M-14 rifles with exception of four, two men teams. They carried M60 machine guns. They carried them during the day on short- range recon patrols. At night they were in fixed positions for perimeter defense. The mortars were set in each corner of the perimeter with loads of fragmentation grenades and various ordinances for the mortars piled in these corners. In the very center of the hill was a communications bunker called a command center. Just a few feet down the hill barbed wire was strung completely around the perimeter. German concertina wire was strung through it and fragmentation grenades and flares hooked to the wire. Just below that (barely visible) were claymore mines small square things covered in plastic seemingly harmless at first glance. Inside the plastic covering was ball bearing looking balls of steel or lead in the front and a square of C-4 plastic explosives approximately 12 inches high, 23 inches long, and ½ inch thick in the back, They were fired electrically. The claymore mines were strategically placed at varying intervals forward of our position facing outboard.

When armed the wiring was strung back to our positions.

I could see the people I knew somehow were Marines. But for some odd reason they could not see me. I tried hard to wake up, but I was not asleep and this was not a dream. Was I dead, or was I visiting this in my mind? I could not shake it. I did not know where I was or how I got there. Somehow I instinctly knew it was not a good place to be or a good time to be there.

I heard a radio and the announcer was saying, "This is Warrant Officer Dale Dye coming at you from Armed Forces Radio", and then I heard this crazy sounding guy on the radio saying," Good Morning Vietnam!" I saw some signs and a radioman with a beret and a patch that said 1st Recon Swift, Silent, and Deadly on it. It had a picture of a skull, half wing, k-bar knife and a partial scuba man on it. How the hell did I get here and why? It was blazing hot God was it hot. I overheard someone say it was 110 in the shade. I did not see any shade other then some ponchos stretched over the hole between the sand bag bunkers and the other side of the hole. It was a desolate hill with no plant life and appeared as though some type of incendiary device had burned it off. I could tell I did not like this place at all; I was ready to leave when I heard someone tell one of the guys to pass the word to hunker down. We would be here another two weeks as S-2 had extended us again! This was not my idea of a vacation to the exotic Far East! The day slowly began to turn to night (oh so slowly) and it did start to cool down a little. This as with everything else I had recently experienced would be a mixed blessing, it would get cooler, but then all hell would break out soon and there was nothing I could do about it. I could tell it would not be very cool for long since all the guys began to get into their perimeter positions to clean and prepare their weapons for the nights festivities. As darkness set in there was small arms fire; people outside the perimeter firing rounds (bullets) into the perimeter. This was common and occurred every -night, it was called harassment fire; to me it was scary as hell, maybe this was hell!

The intensity of the small arms fire continued to increase as the night went on. Around 2 am or 3 am in the morning we began to receive mortar fire, that meant they were closer, basically in our back pocket. It would not be long until a force would attempt to overrun us and they had a take no prisoner attitude. Every man would be dead; they would kill every person on that hill if they were successful. The strong smell of hashish began to inundate the area and finally we could see flashes of the enemy as they began to set off flares. They were so high, they would send one person forward to lay down on the wire, the rest would then run over top of them as we began to kill one after another and they would fall to their death, some attached to landmines which would explode and entire areas of the perimeter would be blown out for more of them to enter. There was blood, guts and body parts everywhere and the stench of burning flesh from the fire breathing tanks attached to a gun designed to spray this gaseous fire over them. The mixture was similar to soap powder and gasoline; the soap powder substance would hit the flesh of these enemy soldiers and continue to burn down through the bone. As the flames shot out the air around it would be completely sucked out of the area and people would literally suffocate as they exploded in fire. God, the smell of the burning flesh was absolutely sickening, nauseating, and putrid, it would remain in your nostrils long after the burning stopped. It remains to this day a smell like no other and years later you would still smell it in your nightmares, always just before the demons of the past would enter my dream world. The worst was yet to come and with the increase in the number of dead and burning mutilated bodies it became abundantly clear we were in all probability not getting out of here alive, but then was I alive anyhow or was I in the dream world just outside of reality or a ghost and dead already? I began to realize it was far worse to see impending dome and be able to do nothing about it, just watch as young men were about to be slaughtered for no real reason other then make someone else rich but believing beyond belief that they were there to serve the needs of our God and Country. Young men full of ambition and just beginning to start their lives with hopes of the future accomplishments and achievements, men that were soon to be dead, maimed or vegetables before they even began their adult lives. Worse yet was seeing the youthful me about to be wounded or killed. I had no idea what to expect or what was right or wrong. Yet they were proud, as was I, to serve not knowing that at any given point in their lives if they failed to perform or act as mainstream society dictated they could have their freedom taken away with the stroke of a pen by one man. We call ourselves a democracy but truth be known there is no democracy, only folks that think they live in a democracy.

Finally it happened, the enemy broke through and they began killing one by one and walking over them stabbing them with bayonets, and I could do nothing except watch and cry. But the sick part was as I cried I found I had no tears so the cleansing could not be accomplished. Here I was somewhere between reality and dream- world, somewhere else. For now for this group of young men the war was over, and they would now be privy to the great unknown, the unknown of what lay on the other side, what was at the end of this journey! Maybe it was like the ocean and the end of the world, we just think if we go too far we will fall off the end and cease to be, but in actuality it will also be like the ocean and we will go to the edge and find there is no edge, just like life, we die to come alive in a different world, or do we just change and become different people.

Before I could drink in all the death and dying I was whisked off to another place. I would no longer be able to see life as I had seen it before, my eyes were filled with death and dying, I would never be the same again nor would anyone else who had seen such utter devastation and destruction.

Death Of A Bird And Its Youth

This time as I gained my bearings or whatever it was, I could see I was on a helicopter, there was laughter and the music was blaring sixties songs. The ones that I heard at the time were, We got to get out of this Place and one two three what are we fighting for don't ask me cause I don't give a damn next stop is Vietnam. There were two door gunners; each one of them had an M-60 machine gun. One on each side of the helicopter aiming out the side windows downward, they were firing rounds off like a cow pissing on a flat rock. I could see people on the ground running in every direction, total chaos, there were children and women, women carrying babies and every man they came across. It seemed horrific, but in my mind I knew war was hell and we as Americans try to glorify it in movies and at the cinema but, by day they would be friendly farmers and night time would turn them into Viet cong just like how the movies portray men turning into ware wolves or vampires.

The helicopters would swoop down to collect the bodies of the wounded and dead. They would be thrown in the helicopters as rapidly as they possibly could so the choppers could began the rise as soon as they set down, they could not sit long before they were targets and easy targets at that. There was blood and diesel fuel everywhere, it covered the floor of the helicopter and people were slipping and sliding all over the inside, they had to actually tie themselves to the inside so they would not slide out the rear because of the slippery blood and fuel mixture all over the floor. There seemed to be no shedding of tears for the dead and wounded, the folks in the birds were numb, they had seen and handled so many dead and dying it was common- place, the norm. The average age of the crew was nineteen. Young men, old before their time forced to grow up without the fun times of those who did not serve in this environment, these young men were irreparably changed. Because of all they had seen only the mission counted nothing else, only the mission; this was the only way they would be able to keep what little sanity they had left. People were expendable and expected to get wounded and many die, the system was set up for it, wounded soldiers returning was money in the bank for pharmacies, hospitals, and research facilities dealing in prosthetics. Death was good business for the funeral parlors and the Ministers. Folks that lost family and friends would be supportive of the war and believe our government was doing what was necessary to keep the bells of freedom ringing, and doing the best to support and protect the ground-pounders, not willing to accept that this was a money venture and the rich were getting richer and the generals, politicians, and big businesses were all on the receiving end of the financial gain. Business as usual, day after day, young men lost their lives and the numbers rose for eleven years that the government admitted to.

I was invisible, I could only watch and see the pain and suffering, the loss and the waste. Everyone knew there was no good could come of this war for the common man, the lower caste American. This was a poor mans war, the rich got deferments and went to Canada or stayed in ivy- league colleges. The poor were drafted and died for their country. This was way too much truth, way too much for a common layman. Then I felt a thump, the whole bird shook, then fluids started to shoot out the rear of the bird, it began to twist and turn with violent revolutions, we were going down, what about all the dead and wounded on board, they too were in this downward spiral, saved from the battlefield to be killed or lost somewhere in the jungle of Vietnam, Laos or Cambodia, in the rescue bird. How sick this was and everyone else on the plane would probably be dead or killed when they hit land or water or whatever. It was not going to stay in the air, it was definitely going down and where it would land was anyone's guess as it spiraled out of control.

All I knew was this just might be one more crew that would be classified as casualties and see none of the so-called freedom they fought for and possibly lost in the jungle forever. They would not compete for jobs, struggle to purchase a home, have children to carry on the family name, if they made it home at all they could only hope to make the morticians and funeral parlors wealthier. Had I become this cynical or was it someone else's thoughts I was thinking? All I know for sure is it did not nor does it feel good to have this awakening, to see this up close and personal. Young men striving to save others and now in all probability killed or worse yet captured to be physically and psychologically abused and tortured to death. The sad reality is most of the crew would have no information for the enemy to get and yet they would die over not divulging what they did not have to start with.

Finally after what seemed like hours, it is amazing how time tends to stand still when something so profoundly horrific is about to take place and we have no control over it, the helicopter hit the ground and burst into flames. It was too fast for anyone to get out, everyone died, the Pilot, co-pilot, crew chief, an electronics technician, the two door gunners and the wounded and dead, now twice dead. Through the black smoke and fire I could see the spirits of those just alive now rise, it looked as though the angel of death had just walked through and collected the spirits of those dead. Only the corpses remained and they were all charred, like burnt hamburger, and the music sounded off, *"Another one bites the dust!* No tears will be shed for these hero's, these young men who were willing and did give their lives for their country, no one will shed a tear with exception of those directly related to these fine young men or friends of them and their family. Most of our American populace would never hear of these brave young men. After a few months many of those that knew of them and all of those that did not know them will have forgotten them and their sacrifices. We are a society of complacency if it does not directly affect me then oh well!

The Field Hospital

For the youthful personification of me was then transported to this medical facility in Vietnam for the combat wounded, those disabled by disease and accidents severe enough to be transferred to the mainland, back to the US of A! Although it was a Naval field hospital, from the first impression one would have thought it was a butcher shop. I overheard someone say it was 1st Medical Battalion, Vietnam, why was I not surprised as it seemed I was forever lost in Vietnam somewhere between reality and the dream world, and this is not a good place or state to be in. It was for all intensive purposes a form or state of Hell itself, living and reliving, or should I say experiencing the pain and suffering we were forced to do and see .For the moment it appeared to be quiet, I walked around the facility from ward to ward; actually they were Quonset hut looking things. This was odd since I was so out of it on morphine in the real world I would have been totally unconscious as the me that was really here in the flesh was. There were young men lying everywhere, the place was overloaded there seemed to be no space for even the Doctors to walk around and do their job even though they continued to make a valiant effort while tripping over wounded soldiers and guards. There were wards for those

29

wounded, miraculously repaired and returning to their units, some full of malaria patients with vomit and diarrhea everywhere and the medical personnel too busy to even consider stopping and cleaning up. There were wards with Vietnamese locals and this seemed strange to me as they were Vietnamese after all and weren't we fighting them? After all, you never truly knew who the enemy was, they had the Chu Hoi Scouts, known as Kit Carson scouts a term of endearment, they were Viet Cong and some claimed to have been North Vietnamese soldiers that had turned and was working with the Americans. I often wondered about them, if they turned on their own what made us think they would not one day turn on us? America is a humatarian country and did her best to accommodate them and gave them a Honda motorcycle; an M-16 rifle, combat gear and they would go on patrol with us.

It made me wonder that if we had a war in our country would some of the radicals turn on their country America and side with the enemy? Sadly enough I think the answer would be an absolute yes! With all the radicals we have, you can pretty much bank on it. Some were really good and saved many a Marine's life, they could see a booby trap a mile away, of course they had probably set many of them, and I personally got close to one of them, not in this dream world or whatever it was but in the real world as I knew it at the time. His name was Phuong, we called him," Monkey man", he was able to climb a tree faster then any man I had ever seen, it was said he had in his previous life been a sniper, and if you ever seen him move it was not hard to believe, not only that but when he got to his destination, he became completely invisible and was unquestionably the best marksman I had ever seen or known.

Monkey man was married and had two boys and a daughter; they lived in a small village just outside of a town called Dong Nghe in South Vietnam near Danang. He spoke more English then most and understood more then he could speak, so he did pretty well communicating and you would be surprised how well you can communicate with someone of a different culture with a different language like the Vietnamese just with your heart, some sign language and broken English, Vietnamese and French. I had to know why he had defected and came to the Americans with all the propaganda out there about us being demons. In his way as time went on he explained that Vietnamese youth had no choice except to serve, and if the Viet Cong wanted you and you refused they would kill you or worse yet, kill your family as you watched then send you to the worst part of the combat to get killed as in the Christian Bible King David did the husband of Bathsheba. The story goes that the American soldiers had passed through one day and that night the Viet Cong insisted that the village was fraternizing with the American soldiers, so they killed his wife and children and took his oldest boy, only eleven off to make him a soldier. Monkey man was so enraged he wanted to kill as many of them as he could before they killed him, and what better way to get his revenge then work with the Americans, after all he knew the ways and locations of the Viet Cong. It is totally amazing how our news media portrays the big ugly American fighting man as the demonic evil and never actually wrote and told mainstream about the inhumane methods of creating an Army the Viet Cong had. The slow but efficient method of committing genocide of the entire Vietnamese race was taking place in front of our open eyes that could not see!

My mind was jerked back into this strange journey in-between the dream world and reality; I continued to be led through the different wards. There were internal wound wards where it would continue to empty out through the course of the day due to infections, dying, and flying off to the USA. Then the amputee ward, this was horrific, young man with every type of amputation I could imagine and some more then I could imagine. Finally I made my way to the Operating area, the place where it all happened, the proverbial heart of the Hospital. Helicopters would arrive, the people would be unloaded and laid outside, a team was designated to tag the ones that were salvageable and could be saved and the ones that were living dead, this was called the triage team. They would separate them and let the one group die and try to save the other, there was just not enough space or time or medical personnel and equipment to try to save them all. Initially it seemed like they were playing God making a determination on who they would save and who they would let die. I began to realize they had been doing this so long with so many patients they knew who was too far gone to help medically and not loose a chance to save someone that could be saved based on their personal experience. No matter how you looked at it there was still sadness about having to make these type choices not knowing the person or anything about them in a matter of a few minutes or seconds. It was imperative that they utilized their resources in the most efficient manner possible. As night fell, there were waves and waves of dead and wounded being brought in and dropped off as the helicopters would go refuel get patched up and go again, the wave seemed endless and the dead would just pile up. The Doctors worked straight through as much as twenty-four hours straight trying to save these people working with primitive medical equipment, shortages of qualified medical personnel and horrific working conditions. There was young Corpsman having only the knowledge taught them in Corps school actually performing major surgical procedures. I overheard one man ask one of the doctors what are we going to do with all the dead as they were starting to pile up and smell, the Doctor told him hold your nose and keep stacking them until we can get a bird for graves registration in the morning after all they were no longer in a hurry and would not care either way. The war was over for them. It was organized chaos the way the sections were run, they would go through triage and determine if they were going to live or die, then the uniforms were cut off and a mop with what appeared to be wiskadene, an iodine solution, was mopped over the bodies of the wounded, then they were sprayed with a hose, by now I was in total shock. They were placed on metal beds: operating tables: one after the other was rolled in and operated on, then rolled out to a ward based on whatever the type injury was and how soon they needed to be medically evacuated to another hospital back in the World (America)! In this hot, humid and during the rainy season miserably wet environment infection was a serious issue and needed to be carefully monitored especially in open wounds like stomach wounds.

And the beat goes on!

Then in one area there were the ones listed as having a million dollar wound, the ones that were not life threatening, but would render a person useless in combat so they were sent back to the world! They had their own unit it was a unit that emptied daily and refilled daily. Missing fingers, hands, arms, and legs mostly. Nothing internal other then nerve damage or reoccurring Malaria. These were the ones that would go back to the states and given credit for their tour in country, and if they had nine months, they got credit for a complete tour even though they never completed it. Mostly they would end up in Hospitals near their home-towns so their families could visit if they had anyone to visit them. This is the way the military had it planned, but that does not mean it always worked out that way.

Base Camp In The Rear
With The Beer

ase Camp for 1st Recon was in Danang, just outside the City of Danang proper. Of course, the city was off limits for enlisted military personnel. This had to be 1968 or 1969; there were QC's the Vietnamese Police posted on the entry gates to the city. There was a constant flow of both military and civilian vehicles and pedestrians traveling through the gate of what was known as four corners. There was a very large fence that run the entire perimeter of the village on the military base side, I am not sure if it was to keep the Vietnamese in or the military out. The women all began to look good no matter what age or how ugly they really were, after a few months in the bush, a couple of beers, they were fine looking women, and god knows they could spit the beetle nut juice as far as most GI's could spit their tobacco juice and that made them special prizes especially to some of the southern boys, me being one of them, they did it while squatting on their heels with knees bent and feet flat. I never could understand how they could do that for hours on end, but being from Kentucky, we wore cowboy boots and it would be hard to squat in them. Somehow I found myself in a guard shack, it was basically a lean to and had sand bags about waist high up from the ground where the guard could lean onto the sandbags and support his weapon so he could steady it for a good shot. Just in front and across the street was what appeared to be a whore house and the girls some very young and some very old, at least they appeared very old as the Vietnamese seemed to age very fast possibly because of the environment or the life style. I seen many senior Officers going into these whore houses having sex with these thirteen or fourteen year old girls, then acting all pious! It amazed me how it was all right when they were in another country and at home they had daughters the same age and would want to kill some young boy for getting into their daughters panties. We seem to live our lives with double standards. They would haunt the men on the posts across the street and be pulling up their dresses asking the men to look at their monkeys and offering discounts on short time. They tried everything short of actively attacking the guard posts to get us to leave our appointed place of duty.

Somehow again unknown to me I found myself on the other side and I was in the whore- house, I had a .45 pistol strapped to my side and was wearing lieutenant bars. Suddenly my trousers were dropped to my ankles and then a knock on the door and the girls panicked as did I and the floor was lifted and I was placed below the floor as I seen soldiers boots over top of me on the floor while I lay silently below barely breathing my trousers down to my ankles and no way to reach the pistol. I could feel spiders crawling over my testicles and around my bare buttocks but could do nothing except lay there waiting for them to leave knowing if I were found we were all dead. How did I get into such a ridicules situation and was it merely for the sake of sex? God how sick men are, to actually place their lives and the lives of others in jeopardy to get a nut off, taking only a few minutes and then it was over, cheap sex, leaving you feeling good for a few more minutes before wanting more. I could see rats, rats everywhere, GOD! When would these soldiers leave? Then I could see through the small crevices in the floor, the girls were giving oral sex to these soldiers, and here I was stuck in the floor, or was I actually stuck in this place of reality and the dream world was this real or imagined? The fear seemed real enough. But was there anything else real about it? Was I even real? Finally it was over and all I can remember or knew was I was running, running, from what or to what I do not know, what would happen If I were caught?

Then in the blink of an eye I found myself at the club drinking warm beer singing chug a lug songs and chugging beers with the guys. I don't know where the running stopped and the sitting in the club drinking started, it just happened. I looked around and I was standing by a rack, (military slang for bed) in a Quonset hut and getting undressed to lie down. Suddenly in my drunken stupor the sirens went off and rockets were coming inside our compound. Fortunately I was able to get into the bunker, at least I think it was I, and the hut I was standing in was totally wiped off the map, totally annulated, a direct hit from a rocket! I was just standing there and now it was gone, reduced to sizzling ambers with lumber and metal strung out for what seemed to be miles.

Again the light came and I was transported to another place.

The Patrol

There were eight of us walking through this jungle, the team leader, radioman, Machine gunner, assistant gunner, dog handler, Corpsman and two riflemen. Our mission was to gather information about the enemy and their movement. Some days we would hike for what seemed miles and never see another human being, then of course there were the days we had to constantly stop and seek cover all the while collecting as much information as possible about the enemy movement.

Everyone carried extra ammunition and water. It was so very hot, must have been a hundred twenty degrees in the shade and we would not be able to rest until we were in a safer area, we were surrounded by North Vietnamese regulars, at least that is what I was told, actually I did not know the difference, they were Vietnamese and trying to kill me, that is all I really needed to know! I was informed they were the real warriors, and really well trained and equipped, so this was not a good place to be or a good situation to be in, especially so when there were only eight of you. I could see me, I was the radioman, I was there again, but invisible to everyone, I could see me, a younger, less experienced me, I wanted to tell that me or what appeared to be me what was to come and what was in the front of them. Nobody knew

I was there, they could not hear or see me, (I am a spirit), somewhere between dream world and reality. We had only been out for a couple days on a two week mission, and I was already at a point where I could care less if I lived or died, the only reason I can think of for moving forward was there was no place else to go and the men I was with I truly loved as brothers, and each one of us depended on the other. If one man goes down then it takes two to carry him that means three out of commission, like sharks to blood, that leaves you hanging out there for the enemy to find and destroy you.

This was a crazy war, one our own government did not even call a war, and then what the hell was it, oh! There I go, it must be hell and I had already been here and had no desire to be here again, why was I here, was this hell, you keep repeating the worse times of your life, times no one really wants to hear about, times you don't even want to think about. Times when the world stood still for you and your comrades in arms, times when life went on for the folks in the real world, the good old USA, but for you it flat ass stopped and part of you would always remain in Vietnam, our youth, our innocence destroyed.

I remember when I joined and graduated from boot camp, we were Marines the greatest fighting men in the whole world, fighting men, going to stop the communists from taking over and stealing South Vietnam. We were the good guys and good guys wear berets and helmets, we are here for God, Corps, Country, Mom, Apple Pie and all that good stuff. Then the first round comes down range towards you and you see one of your team members drop, he is standing there and all the sudden he jerks his head back in a whip lash maneuver, you look at him again and the entire head exploded like a ripe watermelon being dropped off a tall building. This is when the reality sets in that you are one of the suckers who could not get out of going, no worse, you were ignorant enough to make it through boot camp as a volunteer, and then to jump school and scuba school, finally you finish Recon school, SERE school and then Ranger School and you are the elite, Marine Corps Recon the elite of the elite.

It is easy to be a warrior in Peace time, but under fire things rapidly change and no matter how well trained you may be, the enemy may be just as well trained, with combat experience, so when shit hits the fan and you begin to appreciate the fact that person shooting at you is not trying to help you but is literally trying to kill your sorry ass. This is when the sad reality hits home and you realize you, in all probability are not getting out of here alive. The sadder reality is you get to where you just flat do not care anymore. This is why it is a thirteen -month tour since the first three months you are useless since you are scared, so scared in fact, you become dangerous to you and everyone else, being too cautious can kill as much as being too uncaring or lackadaisical. Then for seven months you are a good combat soldier, you realize you probably won't make it out alive and you start to feel like you are on a hunting trip and stalk the enemy as he does you. Then when you get to your last ninety days you are again dangerous as you think you just might get out alive and you get over cautious again. Once you find yourself marking down the short timers calendar past the ninety day mark, like 89, 88 and so on you are considered short, and even your team mates start to look out for you as much as possible. You never want a short timer to go on a patrol with you, he will be scared to death, oddly enough that goes for most of the folks who survive the tour in hell. Of course some actually find they fit, it is their niche and they are good at it, too good, so good in fact they start to enjoy the killing and the hunt. I have known a few that actually loved it and would volunteer for every patrol or mission that came up especially the ones guaranteed to be the bloodiest.

Back to Recon and watching the movement of the enemy and reporting any build-up, concentrations in certain areas. Amazing how you could pick up on how motivated the enemy was by their stool samples; soldiers are not real motivated when they have diarrhea or rock hard little balls meaning they are constipated. Then there was the time one of the team members was looking through the binoculars and he called the team leader over and had the team leader look at the enemy, they were taking showers under the water fall, as the team leader looked at the enemy he smiled, handed the binoculars back to the young team member and pointed along the ridge line above the showering troops where the remainder of the unit awaited their turn and watched us watch them, it was a rude awakening, knowing they knew where we were and how many of us there was and they could have and still could take us out whenever they decided to. Had we fired we would have been wiped from the face of this earth, as we were so overwhelmingly outnumbered. I say we, but reality is I was there in a dream or something, no one could see me and I did not exist, at least in the eyes and minds of the currently living.

The more you work fighting an enemy, the more you can hate them, but learn to respect them at the same time. In order to defeat an enemy you must first respect them, know their abilities and limitations and if they learn yours first they will ultimately win, either on the battlefield or through

politics, the same politics that were eroding back home and
had been for some time. The kind of politics that got us
into this God forsaken war and would prevent us from
taking home the prize, the win. It seemed like everytime we
were winning and the enemy was hard down and unable
to fight us because we had cut them off from their supply
lines and there communications we would be told to stop
and go somewhere else. There was more then one occasion
where we had cut the enemy off from the Ho Chi Mien
trail; their major supply line and we were told to stop the
bombing missions. This was a funny kind of war, one where
we were not supposes to win or loose. Someone somewhere
had this misconception that the enemy would give up
as we destroyed them through the power of attrition, we
would kill so many that they would run out of troops, but
how could they when there was a steady supply of China
that had a vested interest in Vietnam. There is no doubt in
my uneducated layman's mind that Governments wage and
generate war but if they expect us to win they need to back
off and allow the military to win it, get in and get out.

I wanted so much to be seen, so much to tell them what
I had learned and what they could expect, but no one seen
me, no one could hear me and for this many would die and
I could do nothing about it except watch, and this hurt,
God did it hurt so bad, these were our young men getting
slaughtered and stepping over that fence of what is moral
and what is not, and once over the edge it is difficult to get
back over, after you kill your first, rape, theft, molestation,
and every manner of evil is okay as long as it is done in
the name of survival or winning. Of course winning is a
matter of perception, how can we say we won if we sell
our souls! Then of course death and the assassin are both

the giver of life and the thief in the dark. He is the giver of life since these folks no longer have to suffer loss of loved ones, hunger, disease inflicted purposely by the other side, warriors, of fear, of loss. They become free and they go to their eternal peace, their understood Heaven some man or organization has convinced them exists opens it's arms for those that give their life for the cause.

I always thought being invisible would be a good thing, but when you have to watch people you know and are close to suffer, being maimed and dying and you know it is coming but can not stop it that becomes ones personal hell and I was getting more and more convinced I was in hell with no control where I was going or what was going to happen, Sadly enough, painfully enough I could see it coming or had seen it before, I do not know, I just know I knew what was next and no one could or would hear or see me! After the young team member seen the enemy in such large numbers watching him watch them he realized how easily they could have taken the entire team out had they wanted to at that very moment. Then off they went in accordance with the mission objectives, following grid coordinates without really knowing where they were, knowing only they were where they were meant to be to gather information necessary to the objectives of the intelligence community in the rear. The terrain was rough and it was a task moving through it and hoping not to be seen or captured, after all these were not the most loved members of the Marines to the enemy, and it may have had something to do with the black ace of spades left most often by this unit embedded in the foreheads of the dead enemy soldiers by the killing teams that went out in teams of four men highly trained for one purpose and one purpose only, that was to kill and collect the information off the dead bodies of the enemy soldiers. The soldiers were generally grabbed as they walked rear end Charlie position. Then if and when we were operating with the South Korean Marines they would be tortured in the very special way only the ROK Marines could do, they had absolutely no remorse, and knew ways of torturing people that the average person would never in their wildest imagination think of or be able to carry out. Suffice it to say they were the professionals at getting information from the enemy. As wrong or over the edge as it appeared to me to be, I cannot judge, war is war and there is residual damage that is necessary on occasion to gather information.

In this dream world, a plane between the real and dream world, I could see things happening like young women snatched out of the village where known Viet Cong stored weapons and food sources, and while their families watched they were stripped, raped repeatedly by as many as ten soldiers and then if they still failed to provide information a pop up flare would be stuck up her vagina then set off, you could see her explode from the inside out, blood and guts everywhere, the flesh fed to the dogs and swine, people would definitely start to open up. They say today torture does not provide quality information, but I seen it happen in this dream- world, and the information flowed, the people actually took us to the caches of weapons, food, medical supplies and told us exactly where the enemy was and would be. Again I say us, but physically, I was not there only in some form of a spirit forced to observe everything that occurred. I had seen men taken up in helicopters and pushed out the hellhole of the belly of the helicopter to their death just to get the attention and cooperation of the rest of the enemy soldiers. I in my dream world, or should we say my personal hell, watched as the fingers were cut off digit after digit and another soldier forced to eat them until information was gathered and then when it was over, his penis was cut off stuck in his mouth and a black ace of spades stuck in his forehead. This of course made it personal, there was a need for the perpetrators to be caught and tortured to death. This was actually very difficult since most were like ghosts; they disappeared into the jungle, went underground, and became invisible.

Then there were the booby traps, and they were everywhere! One wrong step and you could hear that snap or click and it was all over, you were impelled with a rack of sharpened contaminated bamboo sticks or a you had set off a personnel mine, one more step and it was over for the entire team, many a time the team would have to move out and leave the unlucky soldier standing alone until he fell and his world became a flash of light, he was blown apart into as many pieces and it covered the jungle vegetation, you could only hope you were far enough away so that when the enemy appeared and attempted to catch the rest of you, none of you were to be seen or heard. Mostly these were atrocities only the Marine or soldier knew about and they would never be reported, but we would have to live with them and suffer silently. There was no way you would ever prove it and the upper echelon never wanted to know about it and they for damn sure never wanted the news media to know about it. War is hell and in my personal hell I began to realize that mankind is reduced to the lowest form of survival instincts and that was animalistic, the bridge to morality was crossed, some would never make it back to the other side again, some would become drug addicts and drunks, but the truth and personal experience would remain their silent hell. People being what they are, people, some idiot would later talk about how you were one of the lucky ones, you made it back alive, but what do they know, they are the protected and they could never realize that you died a long time ago and would physically go on but inside you were dead as those left behind, your innocence was lost and gone forever. It is amazing how thirteen months of your life could destroy you for the remainder of the years you have on this earth. Relationships are never what they once were, love was never complete again as we hold back, fearing loss and through this fear we do not want to get too close, yes, we open up, but we always keep a wall on the inner person making us a rock inside. We only allow people to get so close and then we block them or close them off.

After the two weeks were up, the next day was the pick up, but the helicopter came in and there was no team, on the last day, I could see it coming and I tried warning the team but again they could not see me, why was I here, was I in hell? A blast at the pickup area and bodies were sent flying throughout the area, every last man in the team was killed and there was not enough body parts to scrap up to even take back for a proper burial, they met their maker I would think or hope. All I know for sure is there once was eight young men with eight separate plans for life when they hit the world and now there were eight voids in the lives of those that loved them and cared about them and as far as the military, they were just eight men that needed to be replaced with new men to do it all over again, and still we know not why!

For me the light came and I was whisked off to another area to continue with my private hell.

Corporal Hamilton

Corporal Hamilton was a fairly short man with a slight beer belly and a handlebar mustache that he would only get away with in a combat theater, the Marine Corps is really sticklers for grooming standards in garrison duty. He was a good combat Marine, and he definitely had learned well to maneuver his way and that of his team through the jungle. He was known for losing the least amount of men in combat, it was definitely not because he avoided it, he just always seemed to know a way out. Generally the reason a lot of men were lost is they were ambushed and had no way out, Corporal Hamilton was always checking to make sure he would not be in this situation, I really don't know how he did it, he just did, like second nature or something he was born with, a sort of instinct. I feel confident that a lot of his bush savvy came from his Native American heritage. Too often the lesser experienced leader would get himself into a closed off area with no exit plan and there he and all his men would be picked off and killed one by one painfully, sadistically. Corporal Hamilton use to say he could smell an ambush and he could smell danger and the enemy. I was thoroughly convinced of this after being on a couple of missions with him. Whatever the case, he was good and I was fortunate enough to have him as my first team leader. This would be the measurement tool I would measure all my other team leaders with from this point on. This as with all the other situations and scenarios, was strange, I remember when Corporal Hamilton had his legs blown off from the waist down during a rocket attack of all things. He had been in Vietnam for three consecutive years and God only knows the patrols he went on, they were too numerous to count, and he never got a scratch until one night just before he was due to rotate we fell under a rocket attack and he was asleep in his hut when a large shard of shrapnel went flying through his area and totally severed his legs from the upper thigh down. He was medically evacuated to somewhere in Tennessee. I can remember him begging me as I was standing over him trying to help him as much as I could and him pleading with me to end it for him just finish him off as he had nothing to live for without his legs. He pleaded with me to let him die like the marine he was, with pride and his self-esteem, and I must admit I had seriously considered fulfilling his request but I just could not bring myself to do it, he was a hero to me. This was one hard decision, the man I respected the most, one who had got me through situations where I just knew I was dead, the one that would share his last drink of water with me, now begging me to take his life. I tried to think of the easiest way to do it as I was considering it and would have wanted the same if it were I lying there instead of him, I think, but I could not, I just could not do it! I can still hear him swearing at me and calling me a coward because I would not do it, still I could not do it.

So how was it he and I were here again at the precise time as before. Was I dreaming this or was it really happening? Had it ever really happened or had I somehow just imagined it?

Then it came to me again, I was not physically here I was in that place again between reality and the dream world. He had a team and I thought I could see me in it, but it was not me, I was not here, or was that me of years gone by! Had I somehow crossed the time line of life, or was the part of me that died there still living in this hell?

Whatever the case, here I was watching the infamous Corporal Hamilton give his famous speech, if God were real. This is the one that used to scare the devil out of me! The one where if there was a God would he allow the atrocities you see here everyday! I am God, watch I aim my rifle, pull the trigger and a person dies, a person I choose to die dies. Watch as a village gets burned to the ground, every living thing is destroyed and I made that decision that is why they are dead I chose it to be. If God existed then why are we here? There is nothing Godly about being here to make the fat cats rich while the rich kids go off to Canada and get deferments, get into college and become professional students. Out getting college degrees in basket weaving and the likes or going to graduate school and becoming Attorneys to later find ways of taking everything from the poor. This was a man you loved, hated and feared. He was emblematical of the combat field Marine. This is the type man that made love and hate a thin line, often blurred to almost non-existent. What made it so bad was he was so good at what he did; he could accomplish his mission when everyone else failed. There seemed to be nothing about our arsenal that he did not know, he knew umpteen ways to kill a man and do it silently. He could walk through a jungle thick with tangle foot and never make a sound. The other thing that bothered me was the smelly rotting ears he had strung around his neck, they had turned black and smelled to high heaven. He called them his modern day scalps, it took less time and strung more easily. Corporal Hamilton never talked about his family back in the world, I don't know if he had any, matter of fact no one knew anything about his past and no one dared to ask about it either.

Although he was short, he was stocky and chewed Redman tobacco constantly, he would stick a big clump in his jaw and it would be there all day or until he changed it. He could drink anyone under the table and get up and seem like he never drank a drop. His team and his mission was all that seemed to matter to him and no one ever challenged him, you just knew he was evil and to him there was no such thing as fighting for fun, when you fight someone has to die and that is all there is to it.

I worked with and worshipped him for almost a year until I was wounded and sent back to the states, and when I returned there he was, and this was his last tour, at least I thought it was, but maybe he was there in his death and would forever be doing what he loved most, fighting and killing, maybe this was his heaven or his hell I am not sure.

All I know was in this dream world between sleep and reality it seemed as though I would be here for all eternity, passing from one nightmare to another and living in between reality and dreamland. Maybe this was my payment, living these experiences over and over until every last one of those I knew or knew about was dead and their memory forgotten. Then maybe this was my hell and I would never get away from it, forever stuck between reality and dream world.

Had I sold my soul to Satan somewhere or somehow to survive all this? I don't remember but in times of great fear and conflict who knows.

My First Confirmed Kill

I t all started on a dark night where there seemed to be no moon light. One of those nights you would hear ghost stories about in youth. It was a demons night as described in some cultures, one where the demons actually come out to play and collect souls. It was monsoon season, and the rain would not stop, it was a rain where buckets would fall in seconds, constantly pouring and all our bunkers were full of water to our knees. We were constantly soaked to the bone our bodies wrinkled from all the dampness and constant infections between our toes and crotch and no break from the wet. The fungus, Nam rot, or Jungle rot was so bad it would actually break open and bleed or pus would build up. It was hard to stay focused as the pain was excruciating. It was somehow tolerable as long as we were on the move, but when you stop and have time to think about it the pain was intense. When we changed socks, you would have to literally pull the sock from the skin, the sock was stuck there from the glue like oozing from the rot. Everywhere you go water up to your waist and leeches sticking to the most inconvenient parts of your body, and it hurt and stayed sore and more often then not would get infected and full of puss you learned to just squeeze out and soak with alcohol, painful but it worked well, it brought about a new definition to getting sucked, they literally sucked the blood out of you. Every cut or scratch was a perfect opportunity for infection to set in and that was one of the biggest concerns. Jungle rot or crotch- rot made life miserable but nothing like adding a good dose of diarrhea to it, and that was not uncommon. Then as if you could not be more miserable, small arms harassment fire constantly, this is where they were shooting rounds into your compound with rifles and other of what the military classified as small arms. This was a means of harassment, it was not intended to hit anyone particular but occasionally they would hit someone. That was not actually the intention, it was just an added benefit for the enemy and maybe even for the soldiers, if it were not too serious, it would get you out of the rain for a while and in a dry bed with clean dry clothes and hot chow. Otherwise for the better part of four months you stayed miserable, wet and depressed. I was with a unit called 1st Recon, and we were taken to this Operational Post called Hill 146 in the Arizona territory, a name given by the military for this particular area of operation. It was miserable, and almost void of beauty since it had been bombed, burned and now consisted of fast growing sticker bushes, small trees that stood in the way everywhere you turned and many areas that were void of vegetation due to constant bombing and defoliants, agent orange we would learn later, and we were covered with it from head to toe. We were located on top of this hill that seemed a hundred miles up in the air. We had all the typical set-up, about 25 yards outside the perimeter were listening points, they were manned by two men, one would sleep for a couple hours and the other would watch for any enemy movement, then he would wake up and the other sleep. Although it was taboo and a death sentence for them both to sleep it happened too frequently, rain pouring down non-stop, and the strange sounds of all the critters, before you knew it you were asleep and never knew when you went to sleep. This often happened and the enemy would sneak up and cut the throats of the soldiers in the holes waiting in the listening Posts. Next morning when the troops did not come back up the hill the team leader would check on them and discover they had been decapitated. Not uncommon as they went without sleep for days on end often short on food and water, and constantly harassed by the small arms fire, a definite recipe for falling asleep which would undoubtedly lead to death, the enemy was constantly watching and waiting. Above them was the tangle -foot and barbed wire fence strung around the perimeter with the flares and grenades attached to it and cans attached everywhere to warn of enemy in the wire. From the OP we would send off short range recon patrols to collect information on enemy activity, the patrols would only go out one or two thousand clicks or meters, check for enemy activity and return. The next day a different team in a different direction, and so on until every possible section was covered within two thousand meters of the perimeter, and often repeated again and again to the point of frustration.

This was a night much like any other night during the monsoon in South Vietnam, cold, wet, and very dark. Around 20:00 hours (8:00 PM) human time, we started to receive fairly heavy enemy small arms fire and a flare went off right in front of my position, It was me in that position, but I was not there, I was in that world between the dream world and reality and I was watching me, knowing everything that was going to happen and being able to say nothing as I was for some reason outside of my body in another realm or was I actually there maybe this was a dream of things to come! I don't know, all I know is I tried to warn the body that was me, and it heard nothing, never even appeared to see or hear me. The team leader told me to fire, the me in the pit, was that the real me or was the real me watching a recorder or something that would not shut off, anyhow the me the team leader was talking to aimed his rifle and down the sights was a woman, a woman in black pajamas, as he slowly pulled the trigger I could actually feel the recoil of the M-14 and I watched as the round (bullet) went down range toward the woman in slow motion, time seemed to slow down to a crawl, then I seen the impact and watched as she flew back then forward, the entry hole was fairly small and I seen small blood spurts or droplets shoot out upon impact, then I was one with the me in the pit and we fired again and the whole back disappeared, and then an explosion like I had never seen, blood and guts splattered the area and was everywhere, she took out a whole section of the perimeter wire. A team was dispatched to do a hasty fix of the section or we would never know when the enemy would slip through they were sneaky bastards and very efficient soldiers. By 24:00 hours (12:00 midnight), it intensified and we started to receive mortar fire, which we returned with a vengeance, this was not going to be a night for sleep like so many others out here in the bush. By 03:00 hours we could see the bloody bodies of the enemy everywhere just outside of the perimeter, and at 05:45 they hit us with everything, fortunately we were prepared and fought them off causing many of them to make the greatest sacrifice for their country by killing them.

Finally around 06:30 hours the sun began to rise and when we looked out where we had seen the enemy dead and there was nothing, somehow the enemy had cleaned up and drug all the bodies away, this was their way of demoralizing us. We all seen the dead bodies, but they were all gone as if by magic, how were we going to call in a body count? The Lieutenant called it in as the Gunny told him what to say the body count was even though there were no bodies lying there. It did not make the brass happy if we did not turn in a good body count after a night of heavy combat. After all there evaluations and promotions were at stake and the Officers depended on these body counts to ensure their positions. We did not matter, we were merely cannon fodder, expendable items, replacement items after all, there was always new replacements coming in. That night we did well, only one Purple Heart and it was a Corpsman patch up job and he would return to the battlefield in a day or two. To survive for who knows how long, after all the military actually overbooked our flights knowing a large percentage would never come back on our rotation date as we would come back in body bags instead. I am now thoroughly convinced this has to be hell to keep replaying over and over again the negative atrocities of the war we never left! Welcome Home someone says! Granted good intentions, but we never come back once we have left, too much of it lives on within, and a part of us died over there, a part of us we can never get back, never to be the naïve young innocent kids that they sent over to fight to make some corporate executive happy, and in all probability if all the ghost titles and companies are torn away it is fat cats in our own government that sent us over as cannon fodder to make them richer. How soon after such experiences we learn that freedom is not free, it is obtained on the backs of the working class and the poor caste of our society. Just as justice is for the rich, the poor fill the prisons and the rich Gangsters run our country from executive offices, federal and state government offices and they are controlled by who ever it is that truly controls the governments and money.

Meanwhile me and folks like me walk somewhere between reality and dream world for ever and ever seeking the peace we never found in this life or this world. Like the song of the sixties, I can not remember who wrote or sang it as I get forgetful with time, but the lyrics are, 1,2,3, what we fighting for Don't ask me cause I don't give a damn, next stop is Vietnam!

Again I somehow found myself carried off by the light to another place as horrid as the last place and again I was there somewhere between Reality and somewhere else! I was starting to feel the light source that was truly leading me was the dark light, another oxymoron for the evil light or director. If our reality is our perception then can we perceive in dreamland or do we just keep replaying events forever etched in our minds, like an old record that is scratched and keeps skipping back to a specific spot, are we scratched or broken? I know not, I do know I got lost between 1969 and 1971 as the world kept moving forward I got stuck, all the laws and many attitudes changed but I got lost as with many other Vietnam veterans I work with. Then I hear someone say you are the lucky ones, and as they in their ignorant minds and hearts go on in their reasoning, I just think to myself yeah! I am one of the lucky ones; I get to keep reliving every horrific catastrophic event of the past and the war. I live in my personal hell!

The Temple In The Cave Under The Ground

We were on a Company sized operation somewhere in South Vietnam, I think, or was it Laos, or Cambodia as we crossed the fields and the forests and rice paddies in search of an elusive enemy we were sent to destroy. Here we were a Company sized Unit of about 300 men and Officers to include our Corpsmen sweeping across the country- side in a place we knew nothing about. We were seeking an enemy with folks from Headquarters and Service Platoon who had no idea why they were there and what to do when shit hit the fan.

This was some Battalion Commanders sick idea of letting everyone know in the Marines you first and foremost an infantryman, rifleman. This of course was bullshit since the cooks, supply, truck drivers, mechanics and administrators had no idea what a firefight was like and most really had no idea how to use most of the weapons. This was however emblematical of some of the obscenely stupid thought processes academy Officers had and were brain washed to think and believe. Most Officers are administrators, they only think they are in charge and generally causing some good men to loose their lives. If they would listen to the Gunny, the Sergeant First Class in the Army they would not cause the loss of so many men as they did in Vietnam. It is not so much their fault but the fault of a system that brain washes young college kids and fails to tell them follow the experience. In combat it is experience that will get you through and not rank. Many screwed up ideologies came from the Johnson administration or possibly even before him. From what I had seen and heard he did not make any real decisions, he left that up to Kissinger and others. One such idea was the body count, for some ungodly and ignorant reason the administration felt that if an Officer had a high body count then he would eventually kill off the enemy and the war would end, but that would entail destroying the entire Chinese Army. Many an Officer was promoted based on their body- count that came at the expense of the loss of many good young men in an attempt to make that particular Officer look good. Most Officers with the exception of the infantry Officers were assigned to a combat position for a period of six months and this was to give them command combat experience. I remember a particular formation where a Lieutenant Colonel was assigned to a infantry battalion and had no infantry experience, sure he had an infantry related occupation but had never served as a young officer in an actual infantry company or platoon so he did not have the leadership achieved by serving with a good experienced combat infantry sergeant, at the battalion formation he told the Companies that he wanted to see some medals earned out there when we went on patrols, be Marines and bring home the medals! He was about to get just what he requested, and you won't find this in any of your history books, it is another one of those experiences that keeps playing over and over in my head, actually I am not sure if it is in my head or if I actually, in an out of body experience, revisit it in some sick form of mental time travel. As the unit walked across the expanse of the designated area, troops were sent out to capture folks in the rice paddies and bring them back so the young officers could learn proper methods of interrogation. As should be expected they got nothing of any use, but they did get some false information that led us into one ambush after another, you would have thought we were reliving Custards last stand only it was the Viet Cong playing the Indians. In one ambush alone we had over 150 causalities because of the information that was received, no one got burned for it, matter of fact Officers were wrote up for awards! At least three were for bronze stars, amazingly if it was for an enlisted man recommended for the Bronze Star he would have died in most cases or must have literally placed his life in a position where he should have died but somehow did not. For Officers it seemed they got it if they placed their enlisted men in a position where they were in jeopardy of losing their lives. Mustanger's are the exception, they grew up as enlisted men and I swear by it today all Officers should have to spend at least eight years as an enlisted man and obtain the rank of Staff-Sergeant before he should be allowed to go to Officers Candidate School.

I have known many a great Officer in my time in the Marine Corps, but this situation, this time, when we lost an entire company because of poor leadership and ignorance turned me sour on these young kids who graduate from college and go to Officers School. Too many of them think this makes them leaders. That is like thinking or expecting young enlisted men to graduate from basic training and their Military Occupation School and coming out and being good solid combat Non- Commissioned Officers.

In this broken record world, the dream world I was

revisiting, I had lived this situation before and I knew what was going to happen and I could not get the attention of anyone, I had to once again watch as young men were destroyed before they had a chance to live life yet. I had to watch as the Officers based on poor intelligence led them into ambush after ambush like leading sheep into slaughter. Time after time I see this same scenario repeated, the faces of the dying forever etched in my mind, The cries of pain and the screams of surprise as each one dies a horrific death his life blood drained in some rice patty or muddy ground, muddy because of the amount of blood left in puddles from the young men dying and dead. For what you may ask, God only knows the answer.

On one of the last course legs of the so called operation, more appropriately called massacre we came upon a cave and we entered and it was one of the most spiritual experiences I have had, there in front of me in the mist within the cave was a large carved Buddha, he was the largest one I had ever seen and he was in a cave under ground. There were a couple monks and much incense burning mixing with the mist in the cave under ground. The Buddha somehow looked peaceful and seemed to want to tell us something or show us something, but the message would go untold, after we left the protected area of the Buddha and the area near the cave there embedded in the mountain side was a plane, a fighter plane that was sunk halfway into the mountain side and in all probability with the pilots still inside forever part of the plane in the mountain. It was not long until I seen the rest of the company destroyed and again I could not get the warning to the men before it was too late, so maybe one day on my dream world journey I will meet with them and what can I say, Sorry, I tried to warn you but we were on different realms and you could not hear me as I cried out to you, or was this some means that Satan is leading me in and out of my personal hell! How many babies grew up without fathers? How many young newly weds wait to celebrate until their Johnny came marching home never expecting that when Johnny came home he would be carried home in a casket their lives would forever be changed and their dreams would never be realized like in the poem of the wall where the young wife is standing at the wall and talking to her man and in finality she says, you said when you came home we would get us a home and all would be well, but you never did!

Yes! This is hell, but then I am one of the lucky ones, Welcome Home!

The City Under The Ground

Again I was in another place and another time, lost, but knowing where I was, there but not there, definitely still in my personal hell!

Although our sensationalizing news media never bothered to tell mainstream society the truth, maybe for fear of not selling news, or that it may actually tell the truth and let people know we were fighting a formidable enemy, an enemy that had been fighting for centuries, an enemy we had no way of defeating on their own turf and with the political climate in our country and the influence it had on other countries. We were not just fighting a war, we were fighting the news media and our own people at home that had no idea what and who we were really fighting, hell we did not even know. Americans are so easily misled that I can not help but wonder how we have survived as long as we have with exception of the few and proud that protect their arms and their way of life outside the mainstream and really do not want outsiders coming in, when you get too many folks things just start to fall apart. This has been proven time and time again, but then, where do you draw the line?

Again we were on a recon operation when we noticed that all the workers in the fields would work during the day and then they would just disappear, nowhere in sight, it was the weirdest thing. I was with this eight-man team, a ninth man that could do nothing, say nothing, and just be. Like the proverbial fly on the wall, there but not seen or noticed as existing. It sucked real bad, I had been here before and no matter how hard I tried, I could not warn them of what fate awaited them. This could literally drive a sane person crazy, I was not so sure I, or any of the team were actually sane according to mainstream societies standards, Seeing events that you have been through and seen the end results played over again and again and not being able to prevent the people from repeating the same mistakes, worse yet one was actually you but not really cause you were out of body watching everything repeat itself. Each and everytime it would play out the same way. It was like seeing a commercial on the television and wondering why the results were not different as they had played the same commercial a dozen times in the last couple days and the people always did the same thing, made the same mistakes. Was this some ploy to insinuate people as a whole are basically stupid? I truly hope not, but then I often wonder myself about the protected, the ones who sit and philosophize.

Is Hell a place or a state of mind? I after graduating from seminary and college, being licensed and Ordained, and even consecrated as a Bishop have begun to ask this question myself. If in fact it is a state of mind then I have found my personal Hell. I cannot share it, as no one could understand, I have tried to explain it and I just can't seem to put it in perspective so others can see into my personal hell. To relive a negative experience over and over again and not be able to make changes even though you know the end results will be the same and you have already experienced it and seen the carnage is a living hell, at least in my mind.

But nonetheless, here I was again, in that state of being and not being, seeing and not being seen, hearing and not being heard. We were laying in a thickly covered area watching as the enemy walked by and milled around, then suddenly a section of the ground was lifted and there it was, an entire city underground. There were stores, the mom and pop variety and medical facilities, and living quarters for soldiers and their families. It seems impossible unless you have actually seen it with your own eyes. When you first enter, it is tight, and seems like just another well but farther down it opens up and it is just phenomenal, a complete city right under the very ground we walked over. I would not be surprised if we had not at some point taken breaks while they watched us and laughed at our ignorance, and this is why we called them the mole people. I had seen very large areas under ground before coming from Kentucky, matter of fact there was a place in Kentucky called Mammoth Cave where there was an entire lake under the ground and the fish had actually adapted and were blind. No one would ever really believe it unless they had seen it for themselves. There was more then adequate space for a hospital and everything else, and the beauty was the temperature would always remain the same year- end and out. No need for heating or air conditioning. People were constantly getting lost in mammoth cave as I grew up, and search parties would have to go in and find them. It was always rumored to go back to the prehistoric days, but who really knows. The Vietnamese had been fighting for centuries so they had more then enough time to adjust as a warring nation and establish these underground cities and base camps. The entry ways were so well hidden if you did not know what you were looking for you would never find it and often when you did it was heavily booby-trapped and if not disarmed first would be the end to who ever was not welcome. We were lucky, apparently the group that had entered went in to replenish supplies and come out again so we were able to get a good look before calling in artillery. We would later learn that they were so well dug in that even our artillery would not penetrate far enough to cause damage. The cities were reinforced and solid since they were use to being bombed. They can say anything they want about this enemy, but they were good, and as mentioned had many years of training, most growing up in a war within their homeland. The areas were so well guarded that they would know you were coming into the area before you even got there, the trees were teaming with enemy soldiers and sappers. They would fire harassment fire at you over a mile before you got near the entry for the underground city. Generally the area just before the area where the entry would be located would be cleared and there would be no way of sneaking in no matter how good you thought you was. The closer you got the more dangerous it became with punji pits and big grates with bamboo sticks sharpened and attached with poison and often human waste on them. Some of the biological warfare was as old as mankind itself. As I thought about it I realized mankind had truly not developed very far when it came to caring about each other, after all, greed still dominated. The accomplishment of the mission was what we would consider significant, as we got in and out with all of us in tact and left no one behind for this particular mission on this particular day, we would consider it a success. We called in a firing mission and a scrapping run from the jets and felt all was well, a target destroyed! When we returned, we would learn that there was no serious damage done to the underground city, and business went on as usual with even more security around the perimeter. It would become virtually impenetratable. Somehow the Commanders and our intelligence called it a success; I guess they measured success different then we as ground- pounders did. The unit returned to their area and I was somehow swooped off to another little part of my personal hell!

Cat Fishing

First Platoon Alpha Team was going out on an operation/ mission; they were to hook up with a recon team of South Korean Marines for this combined Operation. This team was for some odd reason comprised of mountain rednecks from Kentucky and Tennessee. The team leader, a kind of squirrelly looking guy said we would go out catching and cleaning catfish. I had no idea what this meant even though I was from Kentucky. Maybe it was because I was not from the mountains, them Appalachian folks were a hair or two outside of the cross hairs, if you catch my drift, but I could not conceive any way they would be able to fish in this tropical jungle. Their team was a man short and I had a good reputation so I was invited along on this mission, as though I had an option of going or not since it was the Platoon Sergeant and Chief Scout that invited me.

The team joined up with the ROK Marines and off they went into the bush in search of information. This would definitely be an interesting mission, none of the phony news reporters sensationalizing how evil our side was to the poor enemies. They were only cutting off penises and sticking them in the mouths of our soldiers and leaving them mutilated and dead in the middle of the roads, in villages, and where ever they could get the most exposure. This was them pencil dick motherfuckers means to humiliate our good men.

Atrocities committed by the enemy against our troops were unimaginable to the general American public, as the news people never reported these, only the things we did to the enemy. That sold newspapers and news rags across the country that is all that mattered to the news giants, money, and money made off the bloodshed of our young soldiers. The war was unpopular and the media fed this fury of unpopularity, after all they were the very ones that sold this gullible society of ours the ideology that it was unpopular, again a means to make them more money. This way the media could stay here, attack the government, people in the military and stay out of harms way and sell sensationalized news. Not real truth, or even partial truth, pure bullsit, bullshit a sick country bought into. Reality is the truth was harder to believe then the lies, especially when you lived through it or maybe we just leave it as experienced it. After all it only affected a certain caste of our society and many of us were ignorant enough to still believe it was all about God, Corps, Country, Apple pie and mom. We were the greater cause and would serve in the name of God to free an oppressed people and stop the counter insurgency of communist forces in Southeast Asia. Even if they did not know they were oppressed and needed communism to be stopped or slowed down. Meanwhile our young men were coming home mutilated, missing limbs, in body bags and psychologically damaged for life, according to mainstream society and the news media we were the lucky ones, free to live it over and over for all time, our personal living Hell! Good Morning Vietnam!

Meanwhile battle and animalistic instincts prevail we all learned a new way of gathering information, cat fishing! This is where a enemy soldier or civilian, hard to tell the difference in most cases, friendly by day and enemy by night, would be tied to a tree, then questions asked of them, if they failed to answer or did not say what we wanted to hear the skinning process would begin. The Enemy would be tied to a tree or staked to the ground and literally be skinned like a common catfish, the pain would be so excruciating that they would give up the ghost, die from the pain and if they lived the infection would get them in no time. This was almost an art form, a sick one mind you, but to be able to skin a man without going deep enough to kill him right away took skill and knowledge.

Here I was watching and being able to do nothing about it, I was there, but not in body. I had been there and I could see the body that was suppose to be me with the team, but I was out of body watching. Which was the real me? It happened over and over again, I was seeing it and the results would always be the same, torture and death. Was this justified if the enemy was doing as bad or worse to you? How do you fight a clean war? To win you must be as evil as the enemy themselves itself, if not more so. Then again, just maybe we were never meant to win from the start. Maybe it is as the Peter, Paul and Mary version of the song Master Jack, it's a strange, strange world we live in Master Jack, No hard feelings, I'll never look back, It's a very strange world we live in Master Jack!

It is hard to see a skinned human being as the blood is pouring out all over the body and his red raw body goes through intense pain and shock every time the wind blows or something touches his body and the flies are blowing the flesh leaving eggs that will soon be maggots all over the bloody body of this once human being that now looks like raw hamburger standing tied up to the tree or staked to the ground with ants crawling over the bloody carcass, no longer human in it's appearance. You can hear the screams of the person, blood curdling screams, screams that will live with you a lifetime, death screams distinguishable from all the other screams you will ever hear for the rest of your life. Sure you did not do it but you stood by and observed while it was being done and make snide little stupid sick statements and jokes. And somewhere during the commotion you voluntarily became an active participant of it. In the back of your mind you hear the song, and the beat goes on it somehow plays over and over for just this special occasion deep in the back of the sick mind. It is a song from two Peace Marchers of the sixties, Sonny and Cher. The beat goes on and the information you just gathered saves the lives of at least forty-five men the ones that would have been on patrol in an area we found was a Viet cong strong hold. The means, horrific but the information was solid. Death had become a friend and a way of life, you became masters at giving death and courageous enough to readily accept death, it just did not matter as long as it was fast.

So you smoke a little dope drink a little booze until the memory becomes a distant thing and ultimately with so much bloodshed, death and dying it all begins to run together the line between right and wrong gets blurred, you do not know when it happened, it just did and finally the line between right and wrong becomes almost invisible in the hell hole of a country you never asked to be sent to anyway. The reality is, you never even heard of this Hell hole as a child, it only changed from the entire area being

South East Asia to Thailand, Laos, Cambodia and Vietnam as you grew old enough to find your friends getting drafted and sent to this place so far away, in another world void of anything you had been taught as a kid.

Everytime you hear the screams you try to make some smart-ass remark to show you are a warrior as well as the ROK Marines doing the tearing away of the skin. The truth is we made the remarks so we could escape the horror we were seeing, like playing off something someone said or did that hurt us deeply and making them think it meant nothing to us. This is another of those places the dream world takes you, and you see this mass of bloody meat in your journey between that dream world and reality. Each time you see it you remember how you would pray someone would just finish it and shoot this poor heap tied in front of you, do the humane thing, get it over with, kill him. You mind sees the now fatherless child crying for the unrecognizable piece of infested flesh hanging from the tree. You silently step off and puke your guts out acting as though you just went to make a cat hole visit and relieve yourself, but the puke was bile as you had already emptied out all remains of food and your appetite was not all that good after seeing this. You begin to wonder where this God of mercy is, and whose side is this merciful God on anyway. Then somewhere in our mind possibly as a form of self-preservation you justify things with your reality being God has turned his head and did not see what was going on, the inhuman, inhumanity, and the animalistic survival techniques. Maybe he even condoned it for the righteous few to save others with the information that was gathered and the end always justified the means. Just when was over the edge, actually over the edge, where were the limits and who established them? It was already established in our minds what was written was not valid over here, it did not count in the world of combat and survival. Now it was different, now in my world somewhere in between reality and dream world you pleaded with them to stop as you knew the long term affects but no one heard you, no one seen you, and no one heard your pleas. There is no honor in war only killing and being killed.

As I pleaded I was somehow transported to another place and another atrocity.

Death Of A Small Village

I looked and found myself on another patrol; there again were eight men in the team. We were to meet up with another team in a small village, I do not remember the name, all I know is we were in South Vietnam, and I am not really sure of that, this meant little to nothing for the average grunt since we were there for the same reason as we had been to so many other villages, I knew from a past experience, in another world, what would ultimately transpire. It seemed like there were small villages everywhere and with each small village, there was the probability more then possibility of one of getting wounded or killed. As we arrived at this village we were a couple days early so we would stay in the village and eat drink and be merry or die trying to! This was a term often used too lightly. The village looked like such a peaceful way of life, no real overhead, just enough comfort items, no television, the people played and laughed with each other, nature and every other facet of their life. In a wild stretch of the imaginable somewhat like my childhood, no television until I was almost a teenager and then it was limited, but we played outside or worked until sundown. They had enough food, what they did not grow or raise they hunted. There was plenty of fresh water, and everyone seemed to be family. Although far below the median family in America, it seemed like a wonderful place to live and hunt.

We posted guards at each end of the village and we made friends with the village chief, or should we say he knew if he did not comply with our wants he and his village would be destroyed. He furnished us with a couple of the young girls, maybe fourteen through sixteen who knows, at that time who cared, death was always waiting with every visit from the outside world, be it Viet Cong, NVA, South Korean Marines, Australians, or us. The girls were stripped and checked out well to make damn sure they had no razor blades up their vaginas, this would totally destroy a good hard on quick like, and once a few tokes of the local opium or a few drinks of the rice whiskey, men were not as cautious as they should be with death lurking at every moment. The village would prepare food for us, hot food, but we always made sure some of the villagers were designated as tasters to ensure the food was safe and it tasted okay, especially after a few drinks of what we called tiger piss. Then we would make ourselves comfortable but remain alert, at least a couple would be alert as we satisfied ourselves with the girls and all that was available in the village. The people were glad to share, but who is not, when they know the slightest thought they were not, would be cause for them to be destroyed, from the old men to the babies, all the living things like dogs, cats, chickens, and every thing else that breathed or grew. Their village would be burned to the ground and turned into black charcoal. Somewhere in the back of our minds we knew it was wrong and we were taking away what little these folks had and worked hard to get, but it was way in the back of our minds at the time, not to come to the forefront until we were out of here and years later, at least for most of us.

Again I was in my personal Hell, I seen, heard, and could feel, but I could not get the message to them, they could not see me or hear me, I was not there in this world. I was in-between, yet there was a me in the flesh, but he did not think like I now thought, he did not feel like I do now, he was a me that had died long ago, a me that I am not sure ever really existed. Young, immature, and invincible he had began to believe he was immortal, or was it he just did not care if he lived or died. After all to survive we must believe that life is predestined to the degree that if our time comes we can do nothing about it, the proverbial bullet with our name on it. I began to think maybe Hell was a confirmation of our past life and our animal behaviorisms, those we had wronged and those that had wronged us. A glimpse at what could be again given the fertile soil. The knowledge and wisdom to appreciate that animalistic person laid just below the crust of loving compassionate socially normal persona. I found everything easy to justify, as I was not the one in charge. I was always the junior man I had no authority, I just did as I was told and participated, as did everyone else. I definitely did not try to stop it, truth be known I was guilty of pouring fuel on the fire of an already out of control wild fire of hate and bitterness, The killing world I was taught to survive in also demanded that I earn the respect of the enemy and my fellow combatants, if you failed to do that then you lost their trust, that was a set-up, waiting for a bullet in the back, or to have your throat slit in the dark of the night. There were a lot more soldiers killed at the hands of friendly then could ever be imagined, or even believed, definitely not acknowledged by the suits in the Big House, our leaders. For the combat soldier trust was everything that is what would get you through when all else seemed to fail. Of course the families would always get the Dear Mr. and Mrs. letter that their son had died gallantly in combat while serving their country honorably, they have the grateful heart of America, the America that could care less unless it directly impacted them personally.

In the beginning we play a part, an actor if you will, but then we get caught up in the act, it becomes our reality, before we know it we are as evil as the enemy we came to destroy. It definitely was not our intention, our intention was to play a part to survive, but it was as though we sold our soul to the devil and got caught up in it. Once you have crossed over that morale fence it is difficult to cross back over if ever. Often crossing back over is so traumatic that we loose our minds especially when we see and know what we are actually capable of doing.

Just as alcohol and drugs lower our inhibitions and allow us to do things never imaginable, when you are already doing things that challenge your imagination, it is far worse, it means nothing to decapitate a person or rape a young girl, or burn a hooch down just for the fun of it since they pissed you off. Sure not everyone agrees with the action, but no one will ever bring it up, especially with their own teammates. After all you were an animal, a killing machine and they were animals to you. You and your team had become a pack of wild animals and that would be what would get you through alive, if that is what you call living. This would be a lucky time for the villagers nobody was killed. Many, if not all, women were raped, but that was expected, it was the normal, and there was food and money left behind for the villagers.

The real question is was the village after being enslaved,

raped and pilferage still alive or had the fathers and husbands of the rape victims died a psychological death knowing they could do nothing, having to stand there and watch and loose face with their children and wives. The village Chief who attempted to serve the men that were suppose to be the good guys, the men in white hats knowing they would be okay and then having to eat the humble pie from his people for all they were put through. In many of the villages, they just want to be left alone and go about their daily business. Sadly enough if you were not a sympathizer with the enemy you were with Americans, so no matter what you did or did not do someone was going to get you. It was not if, just when, people did not have to be guilty of anything, just there, kind of like our broken legal system in America, guilty because you were just there or born at the wrong time or place. A victim of the new and ever changing law still living in the old law and never even knowing the law had changed. Ignorance is not bliss; your life will be just as forever changed or destroyed as if you blatantly violated a law you knew had changed. Death was a normal thing each day you expected and sometimes welcomed it.

They don't mind and you don't matter, cause you all going to die!

Again the light or energy source that was leading me somehow dragged me off to another place in this world in between!

Airbase Security Danang

This was an interesting journey and what I thought would be among the best. It was on the Marine Air Base in Danang Vietnam, it was like nothing I had experienced to date. There were small cottages, at least that is what we called them, with maybe eight racks to a cottage and they had clean linen on them with local Vietnamese Mammasans cleaning the cottages and making the beds, and cleaning the laundry for a price of course. I think it was something like twenty dollars to have mamma son clean the hooch, make your beds, polish your boots, and wash your uniforms This was not the war I was use to and I have to admit it was a bit uncomfortable for a field Marine. There were three hole outhouses fully covered about every two roles of huts. They actually had toilet paper in them and some old Papasans that were paid by the Camp itself cleaned them daily. There was a mess hall about a hundred yards for the huts, and they actually served hot meals three times a day seven days a week. The food was not junk either, it had real meat, potatoes, salads, milk and real perked coffee and lots and lots of fresh milk. Beat the heck out of Combat Rations better known as C-Rats. On Sundays they actually had real steaks, the kind from a real cow! This may seem like a funny statement, but C-Rats were all of processed meat and none of it tasted like or resembled real meat I was use to. For breakfast you had real eggs made into omelets with cheese, ham, onions, bell peppers and other things. There was bacon, sausage and shit on the shingle (a hamburger gravy and sliced toast). This was the life, and if it were not good enough they had midnight rations, where they served hamburgers and hotdogs, this was unreal but I did not want to end this dreamland or whatever world this was. These Aviation types know how to fight a war!

There was a Post Exchange where they would take the military payment certificates (MPC's) which we were paid with, you could actually purchase stereos and televisions, watches, necklaces, and a myriad of other things. Then next door was a Post Office and you could ship your stuff out to your loved ones, this was a different kind of war all together. They had Vietnamese everywhere working in all kinds of services, barbers, laundry people, in the Post Exchange, cooks, grounds keepers and even bar girls in the club system. The enlisted club was awesome, they only sold beer, but it was cold, and they had female Vietnamese with obvious French blood, as they were fairly large breasted, working as bartenders and bar maids, uncommon for typical Vietnamese and actually good looking. Again unlike the typical Vietnamese short with bowed legs, flat, wide, callous feet, and very small breasted. They had hard, weathered features and more often then not rotten, red beetle nut teeth. Many if not most scarred from rats and war. Their language was like a harsh slap in the face, sung if you will and they were not bashful about dropping their pants and taking a shit right in front of you off the side of the road. Because the war had taken toll they were mostly uneducated, and uncouth surviving off whatever they could get their hands on, and if it was not tied down it was no longer yours. Possession was 90% ownership, and once they had it you would have to kill them to get it back. Of course you really cannot blame them as to their lifestyle we lived a life of opulence even in this type of sitting the Air Force would call inadequate, insufficient for our life style, the Airforce called it a hardship tour and was financially accommodated for it. That is why one of the dreams of the local Vietnamese girls was to marry a GI and move to the land of the big PX (Post Exchange) where everything was for sale and the GI's (a term of endearment for soldiers) had the bucks to buy it. This was the only experience they had to compare American life with; their life was very meager in comparison. They considered the life of the GI to have too much of everything, too much and wasteful. This bunch, these Air wingers lived far different then us bush Marines this was like paradise.

There was of course a downside to all this luxury and it explained why they were always building. Every other night or so the rockets would come flying into the compound and destroying building and people, this really sucked, in the bush you would eventually find the enemy and take them out, but you could not stop the rockets by shooting at them and it was uncomfortable as hell never knowing where the damn rockets were going to fall and if it was going to be on top of you and your hut or while you were in the mess hall or at the club half lit, (drunk). Even with all the comforts I would rather be in the bush, I had become accustomed to it and I knew how to survive there. It was kind of like that old adage you get comfortable being uncomfortable, well that is what happened, I knew how to operate, how to function, and I knew the guys I was with had my back.

Here everyone was a specialist, and they did not seem as close to one another as the bush Marine. They were more for themselves, but it was good to see how the other side lived and I guess you could get use to it after a while, after all we can get accustomed to most anything, so why not get accustomed to good things and fun times. That is what makes us unique, adaptability! I guess, I learned a valuable lesson; don't envy anyone as their world has its own pitfalls. What looks good on the surface has some serious drawbacks and more often then not has a hidden price that is far greater then what we could imagine, just like being here, in Vietnam, the price we pay to survive has a price we will pay for the rest of this life and who knows about the one after this. I do know that most of the bush Marines hated it when one of these rear with the gear boys talked about how he had served in Vietnam and had nightmares and all. On the other side of the coin, these rear echelon troops feared us combat bush Marines. We looked different, walked different, and had that thousand yard stare never turning our backs to crowds.

After all is life not a cyclic thing where we die of the womb and are reborn to this world and when we die of this world we are born into the spirit world? That is how I understand it, so am I now dead of this world and living in the spirit world with all the memories and torment of the physical world I just left?

These folks could not understand the mentality of the bush Marines and we could not understand their mentality which became obvious when I went to talk to the Sergeant Major and tell him I wanted my orders for Fleet Assistance pulled and to be returned to my unit. Fleet Assistance is a program where they take field Marines to stand security and give them a break from duty in the bush, for some it is a life- saver, and others a life –taker, you can get soft and when you do return to the bush it is all over.

Well once again my big mouth got me in trouble, here I was in my world in between and I was trying so hard to get the men that were actually in body to listen, I had already been there but they would not hear me and off they went in their own direction, back in harms way. Seems there were openings back at 1st Recon, what a surprise that was. Within a week the physical, real me, of the past, was off on his journey back to his old unit and the atrocities of war awaiting him. Before he went back to his unit, there would be a delay in route he would first go on R&R, rest and recuperation. There were three choices; he could go to Bangkok Thailand, Taiwan or the Philippines. The person that was I in the body at that time chose Thailand as I did when I was in the real world or the world of before, real was a questionable thing. Thailand would be a lasting memory for all of life. All your fantasies would be fulfilled for only a few baht (their Currency).

Have you ever felt like you were dead inside, like there was nothing that would ever surprise or satisfy you again? Well here I was not even really there, or was I, it was all like a dream a really vivid dream where all the characters are real except you, and you see your past life being lived by someone in a body that looks exactly like you remember you looked.

Rest and Recuperation

When we first arrived, we were escorted to a holding area to be given a typical bullshit military lecture on the do and don'ts of Bangkok, which for the most part no one ever really listened to or adhered to anyhow. This went on for almost two hours and no one really gave a shit what was being said, all we cared about was we had reservations at a big hotel where there was running water, and it was hot, there was booze, grass, good food and it would be delivered if you wanted, and we only had five days of it, or was it seven, I can't remember but it was short and went fast and most of it I do not even remember.

I love you so much, you want to love (Baht) me good long time? Funny how love and sex seems to be synonymous. Then sometimes the line gets blurred and love is what is happening with who you are with at the very moment in this very moment of life, after all this just may be the only thing you have that will equate to love before your number comes up, you will be returning to the bush, a place synonymous to being a duck on the rotating belt at the circus that you shoot and get a prize for. What was the prize for hitting the duck? A lifetime of remembering, you have no idea if you will ever come out alive again. What says I love you more then a good fuck! That is what life is all about, the quest to get off a nut, the biggest and best orgasm, and to make it even a better experience, seeing her get off first telling you how great it is and was, hell she can fake it for all you care, just don't ever let you know so, it will burst your bubble and somehow demasculinate you. Truth be known I would bet most female orgasms are faked or achieved through other means, like a good vibrator before you enter her which makes sex more enjoyable as it takes off the pressure of having to get her to have an orgasm before you release your bodily fluids and lay over like you just blew or had your brains sucked out of you. I do know some women that would say this is a true statement. Of course there are those that are so hung up in what they have been taught about the evil of sex that would not admit this or had never experienced a real organism and will go through life thinking this is normal. Anyhow, the first thing was to get a good hot bath, a good drink, one of those exotic FUFU drinks with the umbrellas, after all no one was watching, and room service was bringing it to you, no one would see, funny how so many of us so called men had always wanted one of these really sweet drinks, but was too ashamed to ask for it and would somehow with much practice acquire a taste for whiskey or the like as it was the manly drink. Ones image was very important, or at least it seemed that way from my perspective of being on the outside looking through that glass of past life. Next would be a good American meal, double cheeseburger with all the trimmings and good French fries, crispy on the outside and moist on the inside with tarter sauce or mayonnaise, best food mayonnaise and a beer, a Miller in a long neck bottle just at the ice up point would suit me just fine, my tastes are meager. A little nap, then it will be time to hit the night life, no time to waste, the five or seven days will be gone too soon, no time to waste sleeping, you will have an eternity to sleep when we die or are killed. I guess it is the same you are just as dead and do not have anything else to do! For now there was so much to do and so little time to do it.

Nap over, my friend who I buddied up with on the plane was with me on Rest and Recuperation and we took off to the bars to see what we could find. The first thing was the bright lights and the loud music, almost every bar we went to had a live band, they did not even have to be good, most were not, so the worse they were the louder the amplifiers got turned up, after a few drinks it did not matter anyhow, we were in search of women, not a good band. We went to several bars and felt up a lot of women, I do mean literally felt up, seems like none of them were wearing panties, and this is a very good thing as there are many man-women in Thailand, and they look real good and the only way you can tell if they have a penis is literally looking and touching to make sure it is not tucked. Before we were about to settle in we wanted to touch and feel as many women as possible so we would finally pick the one we wanted as if we would be able to tell one pussy from the other, especially after a few drinks. This experience, if we lived through Vietnam is something we wanted to remember for life, and it could very well be one of the last really good fun experiences we would have in this lifetime. This would be a good once in a lifetime memory for that. We decided we would go back to the second or third bar we had walked into for our dream girls. The one I was interested in was sitting in the corner at the end of the bar, she was a living doll, and I do not mean a stuffed idiot, she was if not the most beautiful woman I had ever seen, definitely one of the most beautiful for sure. She had a thin but not drawn face. It was an oval, Asian looking face with high check bones, completely free of blemish, her lips were full and supple, the color of ripe strawberries, the kind that just beg to be kissed. The eyes were almost pitch black like black diamonds so rare, and so deep, like they were full of experience and deep dark secrets, and the corner of her eyes narrowed at almost the perfect curves. She had the longest lashes I had ever seen and she claimed they were natural, I had no reason to doubt it and truth be known I really did not care about her eye- lashes. Her features were sharp but somehow delicate at the same time. As a young child in Kentucky, I would dream of the exotic Asian woman, never seeing many Asian women until I went on my journey with the Marines. I was always in total awe of their beauty and the way they carried themselves, humble but proud. Well here I was where they were the normal majority and not the rare minority, and I was in paradise. As I sat down with the woman I chose, we moved over in front or the band and just on the side and there was this big statue that hid us and give us the chance to play.

I kissed her and she took my hand and ran it up to her vagina and smiled as she told me she was wearing no panties. I thought to myself, how unusual, considering all the girls I had encountered that evening were wearing no panties, I found pay dirt, all soft and moist. I just could not wait until we got back to the room so she gave me a blowjob right there in the bar under the table, God I can still remember that night. We had a couple drinks then off to the Hotel room to get ready to go out around 11:00 PM since that meant we would get settled into where we were going to be since after certain hours you could not get into the different bars until after the floor show was over which was around two to four in the morning, and by then you were too drunk or ready to eat breakfast. Sex was okay everywhere and anytime, whether in a bar or in the cab or in your hotel room. There seemed to be nothing shameful about it, no one even raised an eye when you walked in on a couple doing there thing, after all they were everywhere imaginable getting it on.

Off we went to the hotel room and I kind of figured out I may have not been the first to be in this very room with this very woman. As we entered the room, she went directly to the closet, reached up inside the closet, and pulled out this marijuana. The marijuana had been carefully placed in the closet in a secure location where the maids would not find it, or so I thought. I must have fallen asleep, and when I awoke there were at least six other women in the room, maids and bar girls, and they were smoking marijuana and playing this really weird card game that made absolutely no sense to me. After I awoke, she dismissed her friends and ordered drinks and food for her and I. We ate as the bath ran, it was hot and the tub was very large, big enough for both of us to sit comfortably in. The clothes disappeared immediately after her friends left as though magically they were sucked off. I could not help but study and drink in every crevice of her magnificent body, God! Was she beautiful! She was also very talented at making her man at the time, very happy, I mean what I say when I say she was good and knew what she was doing, it was obvious she had done this before. She went down and slowly began to rotate her tongue around my penis, and then she would take it in her mouth and somehow use her tongue to massage the head of the penis until just before it was ready to release its juices and then she would somehow squeeze the base and stop it, somehow, like starting all over again, she would then climb on top and begin to ride it. I felt like she was sucking it with her vagina. God was she good, and well trained in the art of sex! Finally after the third time of reversing the orgasm she would allow you to explode inside of her and it felt as though you were going to blow her brains out with the stored pressure of your manly juices. After this you were totally exhausted and you were actually ready to take a nap again, but instead we went to the piping hot tub and slowly slid into the depths of it with soapsuds up to our neck. Then as I was almost in dreamland she stood up and with her tight little butt facing me she inserted the hose hooked to the faucet of the tub and stuck it up into her vagina and washed it out real good, that is when I realized why so many folks take showers instead of tub baths. I must admit I had mixed emotions; I was excited by the beauty and curves of her absolutely beautiful female body. This woman had the sexiest ass I have ever seen or seen since. If a woman like her told me to kiss her ass I would want to have her mark a spot otherwise I would be there all day long kissing every part of it, she was a Goddess!

After the extended tub bath and drying off, she rubbed me down with oils and a good massage, I dozed off and awoke a few hours later. When I awoke she was there with a couple other women, her good friend she told me. They were there playing some kind of card game again, I don't to this day know if they were gambling or playing for fun or if it was an addiction. It made absolutely no sense to me, but they seemed to know and enjoy what they were doing. Shortly after I awoke she sent her friends off and crawled on top of me again and some how inserted my penis into her deeply and then she leaned back a little, I guess I grunted, and she leaned back farther, I squealed and farther yet, this was more then I could handle, it hurt like all get out, I screamed and she yelled, oh! You like good! And leaned all the way back, I thought my penis was going to be pulled out by the roots, finally she got up I got on top and released my male juices again and felt drained for the moment. It would now be time to go party at the various entertainment spots. That night there was abundant entertainment, there were impersonations of several of the popular bands and we danced all night it was as though we were afraid we would miss out on something and we only had this time, we did not know if we would ever see happiness like this again. It seemed like for that week we were happily married and this was my wife and she did everything she could possibly do to accommodate me and care for me, she was like a protective mother tiger. This was a dream I had always dreamed of, I did consider this might not be the only time I would ever feel like this, but the thought scared me as I knew if I held onto this thought it would make me weaker in combat and I would be placing myself and my team mates in jeopardy. Enjoy the present and live whatever present we are in at the time. Think and live only this very moment!

It was a fact that this was a prostitute and she was an actor, she was simply fulfilling my dream and soon I would be gone and it would be someone else's dream she would fulfill. Granted these are facts, I paid her and she took a portion of her life and became my private dancer for the week! Facts are facts, but reality somehow plays out a bit different, Reality is Reality for that very moment and then it becomes a non-reality, it is only a memory and memories are non-reality. A lifetime can be lived in a moment or a week or for whatever length of time, as well as lost, time is relevant. You can never get back the minute that just passed it is gone forever. The only real things in this earth is what is real this very moment, we may do something that may give birth to the opportunity that things will turn out as we desire, but there is no absolute, no guarantees. Everything on this earth is temporal and nothing forever, forever is a segment of time that we establish within our minds. One good example is love, I love you forever, and then one passes and that forever ends, we find someone else. Sure the passing thought will blow through the winds and we will get a glimpse from time to time of what was, but we will share our life with someone else. Granted part of the person we shared our life with in the past will live within us as we have taken that part and it has become of us.

Next day we went on a road trip, and this was going to be fun. It was a fairly long trip but I did not care, we had booze, I had my girl and we had food. What more could a young man want? I felt totally and completely free. I was free! If only for this fleeting moment, I was free! We finally arrived. Where we arrived I have no idea, but it was almost a circus like environment in an old fashion way only different, there were elephants and all. These elephants were actually lead around by young kids with sticks, I thought this odd as one wrong step and the small kid would have been crushed under the mud by the large tree size trunk feet of the elephants. There were kick- boxing contests, and instead of the tractor pulling so common in Kentucky, there were elephant pulls, they were the Thailand tractors and were pulling logs and other things I would never imagine being moved by anything except a crane. There were several restaurants, and they were on floating wharfs, it was really

WELCOME HOME Vietnam   91

neat, but the culinary delights they were serving were different from anything I had ever seen, It was quiet obvious I was not in Kentucky anymore. I must in all honesty admit there were not many Thailand Restaurants in Kentucky, at least when I left there.

I found myself being so at peace while I was there. This is when I realized the right here and now was all that truly mattered, there is no tomorrow and yesterday is dead and gone forever in the past, irreversible. I also learned that it is often best to leave well enough alone sometimes, I had to ask what it was I was eating and the woman I was with told me it was same like me two balls one bat, this did not set well as I began to wonder if maybe this was her last boyfriend. It was hot, so hot, I could not get enough liquid in me, sadly enough I was drinking Thai whiskey and I was guzzling it to kill the burn. It does not take long to get drunk when you drink like that. All I could think of was killing the burn I was not thinking of how strong and the effects the whiskey would have on me. I never wanted to leave this place, it was more peaceful and fun then I can ever remember back in the World (USA), I would have to leave it, in all probability never return again or see such things again. It seemed like that was my life, as soon as I found what I wanted in life, it was just before I had to leave it. Like a good movie that always ended too soon. Maybe that is what life is all about, the proverbial carrot constantly dangling in front of us always there and just before we catch it we are moved to another location far away and then we start all over again! By this time I had learned to believe that happiness was a state of mind, we have within us the ability to be happy whenever we choose until someone decides they would be happier by raining on our parade. Misery really does love company, actually they need company to feel better about them feeling bad or their poor me days. We all have enough poor me to fill a ship, but if we choose to find the positive in the poor me we can turn the tears to smiles if only for a moment. After all if we were meant to be happy in life we would not want to die, and ultimately we know we are going to die, Hell, we start to die the minute we are born!

For now I would be happy, at least the embodiment of me would be happy for a few more days, but then what does time matter when we may not even wake up tomorrow. There are no promises and everything is temporal, nothing of this world is forever, yet we live our lives as though it is forever, always planning for the future never living the present, then when we get to whatever the marker was to retire or start living we kick back and then comes the other marker the grave stone marker.

Why does it have to be that we have all these grandiose dreams and too often things get in the way and we never get to appreciate the dreams we had in our youth, ultimately we have no control! Its our life predestined, already determined at birth?

There was much more to see and do before this brief segment of life was passed, this section called rest and recuperation. Funny how I seemed to have lived more in this week then at any other time in my life yet this was meant for relaxation and recuperation. Maybe because the knowledge of the probability of death was so pronounced and ever present in our hearts and minds, the ones of us that had to return to a hell hole where they were trying to prevent you from making that freedom flight home. Even our government expected us to die; they purposely over booked our flights home knowing many would not make it home.

Well my time to return to Vietnam was almost here, one more night and I would have to return. As I lay beside this beauty of a woman I knew this was the compassionate, caring needing and loving me of yesterday, before I died of that person in that place called Vietnam. I was with her, and this all would not exist day after tomorrow. Again the sad realization set in that this was not me, I was in between the real and the unreal, dream world and reality, I was watching the me that once was, and I knew he was in for a rough time and yet I could do nothing except watch, this was my personal hell, designed and prepared for me alone, there were many such hells for many other people but this one was unique and just for me as the faces were all known to me. There are many that have similar hells with similar experiences, the only things that change is places and names. Each living hell unique to the one who has lived it and continue to live it, WELCOME Home, You Are one of the Lucky Ones! Am I? Are WE? Fuck You! We are lucky enough to live it over and over again? While the dead lie in Peace, or do they?

As I awoke I was off to another place and time being pulled by this strange light, how long would I be forced to live and relive this mess? Was there a time frame when this personal hell would end like paying penitence or would it continue on for all eternity?

Back in Vietnam

It was a strange awakening when the reality hit home you were back in Vietnam, the smells are different and the running around with weapons everywhere what an awakening especially after such a joyful separation in Thailand. I was in love with a people, a country, and a way of life, at least what I knew of it, but what could I really know, after all I had only been there a week, and most of it was drunk so I could not be considered as a person of knowledge or an authority about this exotic country. Home of the Asian women with large breasts!

It was hard at first getting back into the routine of daily life in a combat zone after experiencing such a wonderful life. All the smells of the garlic and other cooking smells different from Vietnam. When I was told we would be suiting up the next day I found what I believe to be the embodiment of me years before immediately drawn back into the combat soldier mode, the kill or be killed mode, the one where you wanted to give the enemy the chance to die for his country, and if you had anything to say about it the most painful and horrific way possible. After all pain is good and excruciating pain great, as long as it is on the enemy and not you! It appeared it all came back as soon as the war gear was put on! Swift, Silent, and Deadly, this

94

was our motto and somehow it became ingrained in your mind and deep in your very soul! All the feelings of love and compassion, kindness and trust that were there just the other day was now gone, no longer a part of these young men's persona. It was replaced with hate, hate our own government had taught us to have against the enemy of our country, respect, they were some of the best fighters known to man and could do so much with so very little. A bit of healthy fear as they had no apprehension about ripping you apart limb by limb and bone by bone? War is evil and he who is most evil wins most of the time, and that was our job to be the most evil and cunning of the soldiers not allowing the enemy to show their expertise. Everything seemed more intense now, maybe it was because there was a reminder that civilization existed with civilized people, people that could and would allow their hearts to show. Then was this reality or was it a façade where money was the root of the heart. Whatever it was or is felt good, and even I in my dream world could feel the difference. This intensity caused a worship of the stick of fire known as a weapon. It was good to you and it would protect you, keep it clean and it would keep you alive. Remove the magazine, drop the trigger assembly, lift the barrel and drop the bolt and clean around the firing pin real good keep the bore clean and free of dirt, reassemble and go for it. A 7.62 air-cooled, gas operated, magazine feed fighting tool. You could easily with a little support of your arm drop enemy consistently at 500 yards. What an ingenious invention for the fighting man. It was very accurate and consistent on semi-automatic, and a bit iffy when you went to automatic, but then it may have just been the jerk behind the weapon instead of the weapon itself. This was your best friend, your lover and your constant companion. It would never let you down as long as you gave it a little tender loving care, unlike people who will at some point always let you down. People are much like dogs; once they get the taste of human blood they cannot get their fill. They become like addicts and "Jones" for the taste of more of it.

The sad truth is there will always be a war and a need for the grunt, the foot soldier to mop up the area and get that face-to-face kill! UH RAH! Kill, Kill, Kill! They taught you well and it would forever be embedded in you, no more fighting for the fun of it, if you fight someone has to die! Not even the friendly slap boxing of our Hanna butter days would ever work again, we were what our country made us, finely tuned killing machines, and especially after your art was put to the test. Then as you returned to the real world we called it, you were useless, unwanted and discarded until another war in another foreign country for the rich to get richer and politicians to get elected or not. What did you earn for the price you paid you ask, the right to fear the very system you fought to preserve, the judicial system where one man has the power to take away all you worked for with the stroke of a pen. The right to have to fight to keep your home and take care and provide for your family as long as some bureaucrat or big corporate person decided it was okay and did not want what you have. Then the right to keep your property as long as some politician does not decide your land is more important to the community than to you, and then if they do they can make you sell or steal it away from you with a vote and the stroke of a pen. Just look at what you earned by paying the price of a life of revisiting these atrocities.

When asked about such things as love, home, and

God we have acquired different opinions and attitudes then mainstream society would ever understand. Love is the ability or willingness to be misdirected, misinformed, misled, ridiculed, judged and made to believe you were damaged goods but because whoever it is that professes love to you is willing to give you a roll in the hay occasionally or makes you believe they are the only one who cares about you when you cry out at night. Home is a place you have become adapted to, be it what it may, in the jungle in a lean to or in a house where you have narrowed your comfort zone to a corner or a bedroom, or sadly enough the local Veterans of Foreign Wars or some such organization where the drinks are cheap and there are folks that have somewhat similar experiences. Hell is what we live each and every night, and Heaven is someplace out there we hope to see one day but difficult to imagine and God well, he or she or it is out there somewhere making the world go round while we are lost in a time warp, things, people, technology and laws change but we don't, we are forever lost in a time we never had, dead from the wounds of a war we never asked for but gladly gave our youth for and then to be forgotten and cast aside like the daily garbage. We, the combat veteran who willingly placed his life in jeopardy are now better off living outside mainstream society in a fortified encampment. The more self sufficient we become the less we need deal with mainstream society and the better our chances of not having our freedom taken away through incarceration or mental health hospitals, I guess they are one in the same.

Mother-Up

There is in the Marines a Navy person that is highly revered, each Marine would gladly give their food, water, or life for, that is the highly respected and loved Corpsman. He is the one person that will sacrifice his life for each and every Marine whether he personally likes or dislikes them. I have personally seen Corpsmen crawl through heavy enemy fire to retrieve the body of a wounded and dying Marine. I have seen them mortally wounded and still reach their objective to save the life of a wounded Marine even while having to stop the bleeding on themselves to keep from dying. There is nothing I could say that would even begin to tell the story of the heroic corpsmen. I am sure the Army medic as well carries the same clout and admiration. It is rare to find a combat infantry corpsman without a Silver Star or Bronze Star and at least one Purple Heart. God must have undoubtedly made a special mold for the Corpsman or medic. They have a special lions heart and a love of people like no one I have ever known. We tease them and prod them, sometimes we even set them up in bars with some of the real winners, but when it comes down to it they are a rare breed and sometimes they are better Marines then some of the Marines themselves. Every combat Marine would give his life to protect his combat Corpsman.

It would be difficult if not impossible for a combat infantry

Corpsman to transition back into the Navy, and especially a Recon Corpsman. Once they served with the Marines in that capacity, they can't go back! They know that adrenalin pump when facing adversity and the thrill of accomplishing what few would even attempt to venture, yes they are extreme adrenaline junkies and they are the very best of the best, the Recon Navy Corpsmen!

Again this energy or light pulled me to another location where all hell had broke out, once again it was on an Operation Point where they had been longer then they had expected or was suppose to be. In their infinite wisdom S-2 had decided they should be there for another two weeks. It may be me, but from the outside looking in it seems we were always hit the worst when we had been extended for reasons unbeknownst to me. Here I was this unseen unheard nonentity again in another situation I had been in before and could do nothing to change the actions that lead up to or the course of events that will transpire.

It started with a four man recon team on a short-range recon patrol through the area know as the Arizona territory just shy of the mountain area and the river. After returning and being debriefed, the team reported a build up of enemy forces along the banks of the river about a click (1000 meters) away. The report said it looked like the whole damn North Vietnamese Army had come together for some mission. This was around 14:00 Hours (2:00 PM) in the afternoon. All seemed well until nightfall, then around 22:00 hours, we lost contact with the listening Posts around the perimeter after a second missed situation report about thirty minutes of not being able to get communication with any of the listening posts a team of four men was sent out to see what was going on and if the listening Posts were having radio problems or if they had been taken out, killed.

It was a sad fact but way too often on a dark night after being on patrol all day or filling sand bags, you were very tired and the troops would often go to sleep and it was not unusual for them to have their throats slit in the dark of the night. You would fight sleep as hard as you could but then fatigue would take over and you would not even realize you were asleep. When the first team went out, after about thirty-forty minutes someone keyed the hand set on the PRC 25 radio and then you hear the sound of AK-47and SKS going off, then nothing, just static. We were all out in the open when all hell broke loose and men were dropping like flies, and throughout the area you could hear the calls for Corpsman up, Mother Up! And the two Corpsmen did all they could to get to all the wounded, but it was a futile effort, too many in too large an area. Out of forty- eight men on the operation all but two or three were wounded and several of them seriously wounded, possibly most were soon to leave this hellhole and all other hellholes. The probability of them dying was greater then them living to see another day. They were going to meet their maker and very soon, probably before we could get a medical evacuation chopper in to get them to the medical Hospital where the odds of them being fixed were slim due to infection and the type wounds. Most of these seriously wounded would be put in Triage and be placed on the dead list, irreparable. It did not matter to the Corpsmen though, they still risked their lives to get to them and do what ever they could to sustain life, for that, one was severely wounded leaving us with only one corpsman to handle the wounded and dying. These were the brave men who carried only a forty-five for their protection that they would never actually have a chance to use as they were so busy helping care for the wounds of the men laying there bleeding, leaving their life blood in this foreign land. I have seen these men actually perform major surgery in the field with little to nothing to work with; they were kind of like the MacGyver's of the medical profession. They used rifle stocks as splints and hangers for IV's and covered sucking chest wounds with the cellophane on the outside of the cigarette packs. I have seen them cut a hole in a wounded mans throat with a k-bar and stick a drinking straw in it to allow them to breath. I have watched as they took their own clean undershirt from their pack and soaked it to cover the intestines that were lying out of the wounded mans stomach. Tourniquets were made of belts and rifle slings. I have seen them actually talk a man out of shock, as he was about to go over the edge. I actually seen a Corpsman drag a Marine to safety while covering him with his own body and then as he entered friendly lines the Corpsman died of wounds sustained while dragging the body back and he in his last dying effort saved this Marine and then breathed his last breath. The Corpsman could cure everything from a hangover to poison ivy, snake bites, ripped off toe nails, jungle rot, jock rash, Gonorrhea, hemorrhoids, colds, headaches, rashes, a severe wound or crack your neck when you got a crick in it, once I seen the Corpsman fix a monkey bite. The Corpsman was the man he was respected by everyone from the lowest private to the Commanding Officer. I have met many great men that were heroes and yet they mere boy's in human years, not even old enough to be served in bars back home, but old enough to give his life for his country. I am reminded of the story the Thorn Birds as I see these brave young men sing their final song and give up their final breath. There lives were short lived but in it a message is given for those of us fortunate or unfortunate enough to hear it.

The Thorn bird lives its life to mate just one time and then it impels itself on a thorn and as it is dying it sings the most beautiful song ever heard and so too do the young men who died in Vietnam, or any war! One song for one life! A song they will never dance to.

There can never be enough credit given to the unsung heroes, The Navy Corpsmen and Medics.

Little known facts are that the entire country known as South Vietnam is only 65, 726 square miles in it's entirety about the size of Washington State and was 585 miles in length and 100 miles in width from the Cambodian border to Nha Trang. It had a counted population of 15,715,000. If you do the math there should be 239,09868 people for every square mile of this country, however there were days you would hump this area and if you were lucky as was often was the case you would never see another living being. There was so much of the land that was uninhabitable. So when you figure we operated a lot out of Chu Lai and Pleiku and the Mekong Delta there was a large probability we entered Cambodia on many occasions without even realizing it. There were no signs saying you had just entered Cambodia or Laos and none, other then from our own military, saying," Welcome to Vietnam".

Contrary to popular knowledge the mapping skills and compass orientation was not an exact science, especially when the one reading a compass or map was a new Corporal or worse yet, a young brown bar second lieutenant. Folks who read the comics section of the local newspaper to acquire information for real life issues, and for the brown bar lieutenant they were too busy partying to have paid attention in common sense 101.

Hello Goodbye

The BNG (Brand New Guy) is always a threat as he is so scared he is literally dangerous to himself and everyone around him and no one wanted him on his first patrol, but ultimately someone had to take him. You would just hope it was not you as BNG's get people killed. First as the BNG arrives in country he must complete a course called The Recon Indoctrination Program, what you learn in school in the mainland is far different from what actually happens in the bush. You can read about it all you want but all that gives you are the basics and most of the time with exception, even that is different. The Recon Indoctrination Program or RIP course is designed specifically for Vietnam and our mission there. About thirty percent consisted of hazing and harassment which some may say is useless, but I have seen the results of it save lives in the bush. Many a night and day went without sleep and this actually had a purpose, because if you thought you would miss sleep here wait until you are on a patrol for two weeks or a month. There would be guard duty and mess duty, and more guard duty while you underwent the RIP course. This was not intended to be easy as the more you sweat in non-combat the less you would bleed in combat, at least that was the thought process behind this.

103

Recon Indoctrination consisted of map and compass reading and triangulation, repelling, patrolling seeking information by stool samples, footprints that would tell how large a unit was and how heavy the enemy was individually or how much equipment he was carrying. You would be taught to call in Air Strikes, artillery and medical evacuations. There would be hours of familiarization with psychological warfare. You would be taught a much more intense 1st aid then the regular Marine since we had very few Corpsman and we would not, could not afford to take them on every operation/mission we went on. You would be taught how to get food from mother- nature and what plants and roots to eat and which ones to avoid. Additionally you would be taught which plants, roots and berries were poisioness and which could be used for medicinal purposes

It was not like you hated the BNG, it was the fact he was so green and being green in a seasoned unit was not cohesive to a well lubricated fighting machine. We were all there at one point, but that season seemed to fade and felt like so many lifetimes ago. Everytime you went on patrol or an operation and returned in tact you felt like you had dodged a bullet, meaning it was the start of a new life. Each day truly was the beginning of a new life. Each time you would look around at the carnage of a village or the destruction done by rockets in a supposedly peaceful area, you would think of the song Eve of destruction, think of all the hate there is in Red China then take a look around to Selma Alabama. Then the words would change to Think of all the hate there is the Republic of Vietnam and read the stars and stripes about riots and demonstrations. Then take another look at the Kent State shootings, then all the while the people talk of Peace and Love for all God's children while seeking a higher power through various hallucinogenics. The part they fail to understand is you cannot achieve peace through growing your hair, wearing flowers, escaping from reality through the use of drugs and wearing Peace Signs. Someone has to fight and some will die for that privilege. The very ones that were being spit at and slandered and titled as baby killers while the current administration in Washington D.C. is telling us if we continue to rack up a high body count we will eliminate the enemy through mere attrition. What the administration failed to tell mainstream society and us military cannon fodder is that it would be a long hard fight before we could kill off all the enemy of other then Vietnamese decent that were fighting for communist Vietnam. Those additional soldiers highly trained and well equipped who were involved in the war of so called attrition of the enemy.

Meanwhile the BNG's were being retrained in the real tactics of this war where none of us actually did what we were trained for. Sadly enough over half of the BNG's would wash out of the Recon Indoctrination Program and be shipped off to some letter company of grunts. In recruit training we were still training to come off ships over cargo nets with loaded packs and equipment into Mike boats or amphibious tracked vehicle, and the only thing I came off of in Vietnam was a helicopter and there were very few jumps in this uninhabitable place. There were several times we had an emergency extraction and they would drop a metal ladder and we would hook up all the time to be a good target for the enemy. This was a nerve wracking and humbling feeling as you were just out the dangling for a good free shot. There you were just hanging out in the open as a free shot target, held on by your Swiss seat

and your personal strength in your arms. You would be
amazed how strong fear can make you. Many a man was
killed while hanging on this ladder and you would have to
literally have to pry their hands away from the ladder rungs
they were holding onto. I seen many a Marine almost out
of the situation into a safe zone when at the last moment
just before they were clear a round found its place and you
seen that rock and roll movement when someone is fatally
hit and then they go limp, no matter how much you liked
them all you think of is you are glad the round found him
and not you as it was definitely a nondiscriminatory round
seeking whoever it could get, fortunately it did not have
your name on it, at least this time.

These were just a few of the experiences yet in store
for the BNG. It seemed like eternity until you were out
of the effective range of whatever they were firing, and a
good safe indicator is as long as the shooter can see you
then you are in jeopardy. If you were unfortunate enough
to get hit while on the emergency extraction ladder then
all you could do is pray and hold on until you were in a
safe zone, out of the immediate hot zone, your Swiss seat
was rope and clamps arranged as a seat crossing through
your legs and around your waist. It would pretty much hold
you in place even when you hands were not holding you
there. When reference is made to safe and hot zone, it is like
electricity, it is always hot and all it takes is a break and the
safe zone will be a hot one. This is just a small example of
what the new recon Marine must learn and then he must
learn first aide since we always have a shortage of Corpsmen
and on a small patrol you rarely if ever have a corpsman
available so you must know a little more then basic first
aide so you can keep your fellow team member alive long

enough to get him to a real corpsman. Of course you always hope and pray to whatever deity you happen to believe in at the time. You somehow then acquire an attitude of belief system like Buddhists, why should we concern ourselves in Meta -physics when there is so much pain and suffering in the world, especially in the world you are now part of. The sad reality is you are often the perpetrator of the pain and suffering or the one experiencing the pain and suffering.

After four weeks RIP is completed and now the individuals are assigned to various teams in the company they were assigned at division and then Battalion level. For the next month life will be a living hell as the graduated RIP person who now acquires the auspicious title of FNG or Fucking New Guy, another step in the advancement of the hierarchy. He will also be the new carrier of the PRC 25 radio which required you to carry additional batteries and antennas just to add to the misery and weight, and of course the PRC 25 was always garbled and often would hum, but one thing I can say is no matter how much you beat it up or drowned it, it would always work but in the bush it was a time hated position worthy of being one of the first ones in the team taken out by enemy fire. This is one of the most frustrating positions in the unit, that damn radio gets caught on everything and at some point you are so tired you just plug through and don't give a damn. If you hit a booby trap this ends sooner then later. After all you know the probability of dying far outweighs the possibility of living through your entire tour. When you finally get to the point where you just don't care, and if your time comes then so be it, otherwise you live and that is cool too, just that if you live you actually die inside anyhow because no one will ever truly appreciate or understand what you have actually gone through and those that do are dealing with the same issues. Whatever the case, you, the combat bush soldier or Marine will never return home again as when you left, you are forever and irreparably changed in ways not even you completely understand. You will have the privilege of living over and over again the atrocities you have now lived through and then someone says," You are one of the lucky ones", Then what the hell do they know anyhow!

The first firefight is generally the most challenging and scary experience of the FNG, this is the first time since arriving he has been unprotected and actually having live rounds (Bullets) coming downrange at him and it becomes a very personal thing when you know someone is actually trying to kill you. In my dream world somewhere between reality and the real world, I watched this young barely eighteen- year -old FNG when shit hit the fan, we were pinned down by an enemy ambush, fortunately for us, one of the enemy soldiers fired too soon, otherwise we would have been completely surrounded and no way out, but he fired his rifle just before we entered this small area where there were rocks on both sides, the enemy had us pinned down in the front, the point man had already been taken out (killed) and no way to escape to the rear. Although I can look back and laugh now I know it was not funny at the time. But this FNG was so baffled he could not put the magazine in his weapon and chamber a round so he never fired a shot in this firefight. That firefight seemed to last for hours when in reality it was probably more like ten to fifteen minutes, maybe less, when the rounds are flying and you are firing back time tends to stand still for that very moment. The FNG was actually crying, by the time he was able to stop shaking enough to chamber a round, it was all over. Believe it or not, many first-timers react in the same way, you never know how you are going to react until you have been tested by fire, at least once. No one said anything to the new guy and he never said anything to anyone either as far as I know. Maybe after this experience he would have his weapon locked and loaded so he could take care of business, live another day and possibly cover the back of another team member, after all that is what it is all about, working as a team each member looking out for the other. Each time gets easier; each time you care less about the living or dying and each time is different. There is no way you can ever go back and no way going back can ever make it all better as there is no way you can replicate the situation, the experience of that very moment and unique experience can never be repeated, it is past, gone forever. There are similarities, but no two experiences or things are ever identical, as that time has passed, we are different people, and maybe because we have had this unique experience and lived with it, it is now part of us, our psychic. That place in your life can never be revisited, we are different and our life is different. What was left behind will always be left behind and I don't care what anyone says going back can never be the same as what occurred yesterday. Once the moment has passed it is irretrievably gone it cannot be relived as present only in a memory or as a dream. You can never reverse the past as it is just that, past, you may try to duplicate it but it is doomed from the start as we were different then, innocence destroyed, It would be like taking a fully grown person and putting them back in the womb, even Jesus told us that was not possible, it has passed. Once time has passed it is passed and we are in the present, which is the future of that past, and not even tomorrow will change that.

In small combat, bush units you really cannot afford to keep shit birds, anything less then quality soldiers/Marines, the ones that learn fast and know how to apply what they learn. If they are not quality they have short tours, or are transferred to another line unit where all they need are bodies. In most cases the folks that get to the level of being transferred to a small recon unit they are fairly well screened until we get the cream of the crop, occasionally one will slip through but not too often. So the next time all hell breaks out this trooper will show his true grit and pull through for you, as stated that first fire fight is a real rude awakening when you start to see real bullets flying at you and they are not kidding, they want to kill you! Many cases they do, but you have that attrition rate. It is expected, no matter how you calculate it, someone will ultimately die. It will be someone in your unit in all probability. Death will forever more be an upfront, personal, in your face experience and you will embrace it as a fellow soldier. You also have that small percentage of the elite trained that just can't hack it!

Finally with a few missions behind him, the FNG has become one of the guys and is now part of the team. This is a team like nothing experienced in the rest of the world, you have passed through up to this point, you have now been tested by fire, these are men that will literally give their life for you, and some just may have to.

Place Of
The Walking Dead People

Suddenly I was caste from where I was observing the new guy into a place where the pure horror of reality transcended the atrocities of war itself, a form of war where man was not fighting man but being taken over by disease and the inhumanity of fellow mankind. A sealed off guarded village if you will where the Vietnamese people who suffer from various diseases like Hanson's and polio and mental retardation were all dumped. A place where the cursed were pinned into an area away from other human forms and forced to live among the other infected, infested, or possessed, whatever you would call it.

This was the manifestation of fear or evil and disease held in an area not to be known by our fine news media a place where they did not fear the enemy attacking, actually it was a house of the walking dead people. This is a place where it was as common to see body parts rotted off as to breath another breath. Many were missing noses and ears, jaws were rotted out legs and arms missing, it was horrible and the stench of rotting bodies is one you will never forget. This place would definitely make one question the existence of a God, especially a God of Mercy; of course you have those radicals that would claim God was punishing these heathens. This goes against all I have ever been taught, I was

taught that God does not test us but allows us to be tested
because of decisions we make or allow others to make for us.
These folks acquired this disease from birth, what possible
decision could they have made to lead to this type test.
These folks were suffering from a long gone disease, one we
had eradicated in America. But this is a third world country
oppressed by seemingly everyone from China to France and
now us, all for the good of the people. Or was it for the
good of whatever country was there at the time, taking all it
could of the natural resources and the people. These people
would try to live life as normal as they could perceive what
was normal. They worked when they could, doing what
ever it was they did for the good of the community at large,
they mated and had children, some of the team members
made the statement they could not believe anyone would
consider mating and bringing another person into a the life
they were living. Truth is who are we to judge, who are we
to say who can and can't reproduce, is this not what Nazi
Germany was doing, attempting to create the perfect race.
Of course one could justify abortion knowing the children
of these abominations would turn out such distortions that
almost simulated human beings but were actually monsters
in flesh not even what mainstream society would consider
human, with rotting flesh. Could we then say a human
brain was worth saving, or was this monstrosity equal to
human and human brain, was it trainable, if so was it able
to develop? Sadly enough the children that looked normal
would also end up with the affects of this nasty horrible
rotting disease. It was even hard for me to imagine a person
slowly having their ears rot off and being able to do nothing
about it except carry on as though this was normal, but
then it was their normal after all, they had no medicine

or anything else to make it better. This place brought on seriously biased ideologies, and after all who were we, just killers and death machines, that is what we were trained to do, that is what we had to do to survive this hellhole. So how were we better then the most evil of the evil, was it because we were given a mission, after all we chose how we would carry out this mission. What was our mission exactly? Was it to sleep, eat, shit, rape, plunder and kill? That is what it seems to have come down to only we professed to be the ones with the white hats! There is a song I can only remember a bit of and it said," and that's me in the corner losing my religion, there I have said too much", and that pretty much paraphrased how I was feeling when we entered the village, they were not the least bit afraid of us, it would be a blessing to them if we killed them. The Vietnamese were like the American Indian in that they felt they were possessed by the devil so they would not touch, kill or even allow them to be seen by anyone outside the village. Amazingly after all the team had seen and was forced to do just to survive and gather information they found it hard if not impossible to look into the eyes of these people, all they wanted was to get the hell out of this place. To the best of my recollection this was the first village we had visited where no one was killed, wounded, raped or even beat up, the village remained exactly as it was when we left, no destruction or improvements, but the psychological wounds sustained by our visit and experience with these people were wounds the team would never completely heal from and would remain with them for all eternity, they were far worse then all the physical wounds we had ever received, knowing anyone of us could be in this same position with a mere infection from something we could not even see or hear.

I was somehow transported out of the village as I was watching the team leave at a rapid pace not looking back and making damn sure they left nothing to cause them to ever have to or need to return.

The Personification
Of A Young Me

The spirit guide, light or energy source had led me to an area just inside the Quang Tri province when all hell broke loose. Somehow the young person that was the me of the past was walking rear-end Charlie, and we somehow got hit from the middle of the team, this seemed kind of strange as we were usually hit from the rear and rear end Charlie was taken out or from the point. The name rear-end Charlie came from the rear man in the formation always being taken out by Charlie the word given to the enemy. I remember watching this youthful me in the flesh as he was rolling off the path and crawling under some kind of tree, I seen him firing his rifle until he was running low on ammunition. The silence was unnerving, then as I watched him crawl out and toward the other team members, I saw an intensely bright flash, It immediately drew me into the body of the person I knew to be me, and I must have been hit as the person from the past was dragged out by the team, the Corpsman was hooking up something, I could not see close enough then I noticed his arm was wrapped and a couple of tree limbs were wrapped around it to keep it straight and a rifle sling was tightened very tight to hold it together. This was I! It was the very wound I had received years before! I awoke in first medical evacuation field hospital. I remember very little at that point as the guide was busy directing me to the other men around the hospital and the suffering they were undergoing as my person body was out of it stoned on morphine. I saw young men with only half their bodies, some with tubes down their throats so they could breath, some with feed tubes, others with tubes in their penis. I saw some young men with half their faces missing and noses missing after being blown off. There was one particular one that still haunts me and sure enough I would see him over and over again, the skin on his face had melted from the napalm or something, it was past horrible and he looked monstrous and they could only do so much surgery at a time, then rewrap. It reminded me of the man in the iron mask or better still the Phantom of the opera, I thought how sad this was as he looked like he was probably a good looking young man before this, he would never be the same again, the war would be with him every minute of everyday for the rest of his life. This young, adult life was just beginning and he had everything going for him with one slight detour that would forever impact his life for all eternity, a slight detour called Vietnam!

There was no shortage wounded young men, they seemed to go on and on there seemed to be no end to the pain and suffering, what a cost for these brave young men, what did we gain from it? When I returned to observe the embodiment of myself much younger of course, I felt it a crime that I should be in this place with all the severely injured, but off I went to into another morphine trip and I awoke in a Naval Hospital in Japan. Of course I had no idea where I was and the morphine was slowly wearing off. Finally as I came out of it in a morphine haze, I had a splitting headache and as I looked around there were Asians everywhere, and the lights were bright, so very bright, like what we hear in the movies as the light to lead us to our eternal resting place. Then all the sudden I heard someone screaming out, Holy Shit! They got me, now they were going to experiment on me! Then someone gave me another shot and I was out for the count again and when I woke I awoke slowly to see Navy Corpsmen all around. I was in Naval Hospital in Japan and was enroute to Memphis Millington Tennessee for the nearest Naval hospital to my home in Louisville Kentucky. I had nerve damage in my right arm, and of course as would have been Murphy's Law, if one thought about it, if you are going to have an arm injured and you are right handed that is the arm that will be damaged. This was a blessing and a disaster, because I was right handed and it was my right hand I was taken out of combat, I was useless to a combat unit. The disaster was I was right handed and could not write, eat, or even wipe my ass; I had to learn to use my left hand for all these purposes. They tried the electric shock and nothing then the pinprick and still nothing. That as bad as it was certainly was not the worst of my problems, actually as I said earlier, this was a million dollar wound, and as wounds go this was possibly one of the better places or ways to be wounded, but there was another demon lurking in the crevices of my mind and I did not know it but I would diagnosed by the Psychiatrist at the Memphis Millington Naval Hospital as displaying signs of Post Traumatic Stress disorder, what the old timers referred to as battle fatigue or shell shock even at this point, my first tour in Vietnam and yet there were two more coming and the Mayguez. Of course I thought it was a bunch of malarkey as I was a Marine and we do not suffer from such sissy things as this, we are warriors! I just needed to get the hell out of here and back in the bush where I belonged.

I in this spirit between worlds tried so hard to reach the embodiment of me but you cannot change history and I could not be heard, the past will always be the past and it will always repeat itself.

Party Time In The World

For now it was going to be party time! I was transferred to this small Naval Hospital in Tennessee and I would take advantage of it. The days were just fine, I could pretty much sleep all day unless I had to see a Doctor, and that was only a couple times a week. I had to see the Psychiatrist, and the neurosurgeon. At night I would be up at all hours with nightmares about my team and friends. Finally seeing there was no improvement in my right arm, I was scheduled and shipped back to Tennessee.

Memphis Millington Tennessee to be exact, it was a small Naval Hospital. It was actually very patient oriented and really went out of the way to provide entertainment for the veterans that were wounded and the medical personnel were very polite and patient with us. I have no idea what they turned the facility into, but after Vietnam it was closed down. It was an extremely clean hospital. This was going to be a fun time. I had no duty or job and every Thursday after group Counseling I would be dismissed and allowed to go on liberty, so I would head out to my home town Louisville Kentucky until Tuesday morning. Occasionally I would catch a ride with some of the Corpsmen but mostly I had to hitchhike to and from. It was around 300 miles I would guess, but I always seemed to have pretty good luck

119

getting a ride. In the late 1960's in the south, military men in uniform were fairly well respected, sure you had a few idiots, but most of them were in the government, for the most part southern folks treated you just fine. I have on more then one occasion been taken home to dinner before they would let me get back on the road. This would last for about a year before they determined I was well enough to get orders and get transferred to a new duty station.

I had completed nine months of my tour in Vietnam so they gave me credit for the complete tour even though it was four months shy of a full tour, but I would show them I would go back and get the gook that got me, yeah! I would show them!

The weekends really were interesting, I guess I got picked up and spent the weekend with very interesting women as much as I made it home to Louisville Kentucky. They would pick me up and they would foot the bill for us to party, they would know I was broke and they would pay for the hotel and the booze or they would even take me home with them and party we did. I guess they wanted to do their part for their country and the war effort. It actually got to the point where it took all week to prepare for the extended weekend that happened every week. I remember one particular night when I was picked up by this really pretty blonde that was built like a brick shit house, she had legs that went on forever and tits that stood out like headlights on a Studebaker. Man was she the cat's meow! I knew it would go nowhere as she was just too fine to get wild and crazy with a wounded Marine. I was wrong, she had obviously been drinking for a while, possibly all day long and she kept singing she had her mo-jo working and was out to have a ball. We stopped at the White Castle and she bought several bags of hamburgers for both of us, (the hamburgers were about four bites if that, greasy and loaded with onions). Then we went to the Piggley Wiggly store and she bought a couple cases of Fall City beer, and it was to the party, at her apartment in downtown Millington Tennessee. Soon as we walked in the apartment she demanded we take off all our clothes so everytime I got hard we could get it on, it was I have to admit getting to a point where I was wishing it would not get hard, I was getting sore, what a price to pay, a little tenderness for a lifetime of memories. Night turned into day and I do not remember if we even slept. If so it was because we passed out and then started all over again. Then as the weekend ended she dropped me off at the hospital in Memphis Millington and I thought I had heard the last of her. I was wrong, she called every day several times a day, and then I told her I had three more years to do in the Marines and did not know where I would be transferred to, she told me to quit and stay with her and when I tried to explain you could not just quit the Marines she got upset and said I just did not want to stay with her, on that point she was correct, as I never seen her sober or straight. I again started to travel back and forth to Louisville Kentucky and somehow somewhere I ended up getting married to this woman I really did not know and after I sobered up I found I was not just married but had a four-year-old kid, I was all of eighteen, almost nineteen. This was a real bitch of a woman all we did was argue and fight, she would literally throw anything within grabbing distance, and I figured I best get away from this as soon as possible or one of us would end up in prison or dead, and given my past luck in life, it would be me.

Back to the Marines

Then as if God had personally prepared my orders for the right place and the perfect timing I received orders to Santa Ana (LTA) Helicopter base in California. I reported in and was immediately out of place in this sunshine and easy duty station. I had no idea what I would be doing since there was no one else in my military occupation, Infantryman. I was assigned to a Headquarters and Training squadron as Training Non- Commissioned – Officer, I was only an E-3 Lance Corporal, I was also the only Lance Corporal or Corporal, or sergeant that had been in combat in Vietnam. I was the junior man in the section and was more highly decorated then most everyone including the Officers and senior enlisted. I no sooner arrived than I began to realize I was not cut out for the stateside duty where you had to look good and that was about it. I knew if I stayed here too long I was bound to get into trouble. I worked hard and I partied hard just like my comrades in Vietnam, the bush Marines. This was a different kind of Marines and I felt out of place. I immediately put in for orders to Vietnam. I was not cut out for this state side duty. All I had to do was monitor Physical Fitness Tests, and essential subjects tests then make data entries in the training jackets of the personnel in the unit. At night I would get totally shit-faced drunk and then have to face the next day with a hang over. Once a week I would have duty Non-Commissioned Officer, which was a joke, I could have done as much sitting at home. Instead was forced to stay at the Squadron duty room and all night I would watch the Cal Worthington car sales with his dog Spot or something like it, and the old movies. Then I was off all day next day. I actually think I was there just to keep the Officers Company that was standing Officer of the Day duty. The young Officers were different then the Infantry Officers, most were helicopter Pilots, and all they wanted to do was fly. They were nothing more then college boys with bars, their rank insignia. This made it easy to communicate with them, as we were both different, they wanted to fly and I wanted to get back in the bush.

I felt empty I needed to get back in the bush in Vietnam, after all this war was not going to last forever and then what? I wanted as much of it as I could get before it was too late. How long would I have to wait for another war? Ironically on the day I got my divorce papers from my attorney with the dissolution of marriage, I received the orders I had so impatiently awaited. I had been there only three months. The folks in the unit threw me a big party, I was a bit torn, there were a bunch of really good people, and we were just different, like we came from different worlds. We bid our farewells and off I went to my new duty station without desiring a delay in route. A delay in route was a thirty - day delay before I had to report, it was to be spent with our loved ones in case we did not make it. As far as I was concerned I had no one and did not care, my friends would be in the bush! Besides, no one would really cared if I made it back anyhow, the world had moved on, I was stuck in a different time and world, and I had nothing to leave to anyone or anyone to leave it to anyhow.

Back to Vietnam

My orders read replacement for First Marine Division Republic of Vietnam. I was going home again; going to a place where I would be appreciated for who I was and what I was good at, combat. I was like a Pit bull having tasted blood and wanting more of it. I would be assigned to 1st Recon again, my old home unit, back to A Company. I was so anxious to see all the good old boys I had served with and could not get there soon enough. Finally I arrived, and as I checked into the unit I did not see anyone of the guys I had previously served with and there was a different feeling about things, I could not put my finger on it but it just seemed different somehow. I finished checking in and because of my previous tour I was not required to go through the complete cycle of Recon Indoctrination, I had a abbreviated cycle, I repelled mountain Mother Fucker and plotted a few drop zones and that was about the extent of it a couple of weeks and I was scheduled for an operation. This time my team would go to Marble Mountain, and all day long transfer radio communications, and all night long we would take incoming rockets, a load of fun and games. This was an operation that would last for two months and it was enough to drive even a sane man crazy, same thing everyday and every night. The only reading material was a

125

Gideon Bible and an old Playboy with the center fold long missing, we all took turns reading them, this way we got educated and relieved, from one extreme to the other. By the time the operation was over we all had the first five books of the Bible memorized. Finally this operation was over, I had my doubts it had accomplished anything other then trying our patience. Then back to our rear for steaks and beer, a week of getting drunk and preparing our gear for the next operation.

The next operation was not to be so boring and I was again in the place between worlds. Somewhere between dream world and reality. I was somewhere between living in the here and now or the spirit world with disdain for all humanity and love of my fellow warriors maybe as Elvis sang, on the edge of reality. Was hell just another name for in a different realm of the present world? This operation was in the jungle and the canopy was so thick you could not see the sunshine. There were booby traps everywhere and you could hear Vietnamese soldiers talking from miles away, which meant they could hear our movement and they knew exactly where we were, we were really good at what we did, snooping and pooping, but they were well trained. They had been in combat since they were children and some for several years; we just came for thirteen-month tours at a time and never wanted to see this Godforsaken place again!

It made it worse as I did not know these new team members, and team members that were not well seasoned and trained could get you killed in a hurry. I tried often to warn the personification of myself but he would not hear and he was definitely headed for the shit. I had watched this particular team leader make the same mistake he was about to make this time, but no matter how much I screamed out, no one could hear me, not even the me of yesterday. The team leader was one of those people that had definitely learned a lot and was good at his job, but he did not know everything as well as he thought he did. Some things come only with experience and too often mistakes we make. Kind of like when we miss questions on tests, we learn those questions we missed even better then the ones we got right. The problem is in Vietnam when you make a mistake others pay the price with their lives. This Team Leader had an inexperienced man walking point and that was catastrophic at best. Sure enough he stepped over a land mine not even aware it was there, and the next man in line tripped it and all that could be seen was blood and guts flying through the air, into and on trees everywhere. Four of the eight men were gone in the blink of an eye or the sound of a ping below them. There were not enough of the bodies to even carry back. For now that was the government's problem on how to explain where the bodies were, ours was to get the hell out of dodge and save our backsides. This was going to be a night of pure hell with them looking to see who if anyone was left alive. If we did not cover some ground and fast we would be prisoners of war or dead, probably the later as we did not know enough to be useful. God it seemed like the rapid movement of us putting one foot in front of the other went on forever, dead tired but not yet physically dead and the only way that would happen is if the pace slowed or stopped. Tripping over roots falling and getting bruised and bloodied up, but it was better then the other option of giving up and getting captured and mutilated or killed for someone else's pleasure. Somehow missing the massive amount of booby traps we knew were there, for some reason God or some higher source had lifted us up on the wings of the eagles. The canopy was getting thinner and then as we thought we were out of it suddenly it got thicker. We were lost in this vast sweltering pot of inhumanity where death awaited each turn or around each bush. I could see the end coming up but they could not, they were just running from something or someone that was chasing them. Finally just ahead we could hear talking, oh Shit! We were close to the talk, then as we draw closer we could hear it was English or some form of it anyhow, we had ran into a platoon of Australian Marines. This was a real surprise since I never even knew the Australians were involved in this war, but they were some type of Australian Special Forces I was informed.

We would be safe now, they fed us, gave us drink and we rested as they got hold of the medical evacuation folks and had us airlifted out and returned safely back to our command. We were bruised, beat up and totally exhausted, but we were now safe and could truly rest. I never thought I would be so happy to see a bunch of Aussies in my life! To this day I know we owed our lives to those Aussies, so all I can say is Thanks Mate!

After we had rested up a bit the hard reality hit home, four young men had lost their lives. The Commanding Officer would have another four letters to write home to Mothers of young American Marines, telling how their young children or Fathers of young children and husbands of young wives had served gallantly and gave their lives for their country, and oh! By the way the bodies would not be returning. Only fragments and truth be known they would never even distinguish who was who, just scrapes of what once was a vibrant human being in the prime of his life. Of course we, the experienced combat veterans all knew they had died because one point man was careless and not savvy enough to have been in the position as point man. Only us savvy enough to have survived the experience of the living jungle of death would ever know the truth. Even the trees had eyes in this living jungle of booby traps and land mines as well as every manifestation of crawling, flying, and swimming creature meant to make life miserable, and that was not to mention the enemy troops. The government and the Marine Corps, the unit, trying to comply had rushed these young men into a position they were not prepared for or able to do. They would go home all properly designated as heroes who gave their lives for a proud country that in all honesty could care less about these young men as long as they were not their young men. They would have their Purple Hearts proudly presented to the family posthumously as some form of justification for the loss to the family of these young men. They would never truly know how and why these young men had to die in a country halfway around the world that none of us had even heard of only a decade or so earlier. All the ceremonial formalities would be given and in another place on another day other young men barely out of adolescence would be killed and someone else would write a letter and another Purple Heart with the loss of another life. Then we must remember they were expendable and only useful to fulfill the needs of the war effort, that we had no way of winning in the political realm at the time in history. The sun still would shine the next day and the moon would still come up at night, life would go on as before and in a year the only ones that would remember these men would be their immediate family, and those that served in the living hell with them. They just did not matter; they were collateral damage to support the war effort. Then the reality of life hits you right between the eyes life in general does not matter, just another mouth, another number that will someday expect a social security check and before that need medical care and maybe a job. They would grow and have kids, the ones who made it back walk the earth as a combat zombie, a wounded warrior, a piece of us died inside, another someone that has learned the truth and that is we are only free to think we are free, freedom exists as long as we do not know too much, ask too many questions or expect too much and it matters little how much good you have done, as one oh shit! Negates every bit of it. You are judged on only the issue at hand and not all the good you have tried to do. The best we could hope for is to somehow move forward and deal with what we had experienced that if we tried to explain no one except another combat veteran would ever understand. Most of the folks we knew including our own children just did not care about knowing what happened in Vietnam. Then if we have a successful life we would leave as we entered, bald, no teeth, incontinent, and wrinkled with a feeble mind and barely if at all be able to talk.

Here in the valley of death all that truly matters is the right here and the right now, there was no yesterday, as that can cause remorse and pain which makes you an easy target, there is no tomorrow, only today over and over and over again!

Again I was whisked away by this energy source or light and found myself in another of the past experiences again. Was this hell and if so was I doomed to continue this journey for all times, eternity? When would it end?

Combined Action Program

Ifound myself watching as two fields Corpsman, a Chaplain, Medical Doctor and a four-man team of armed guards administered medical aid to a small village. These were same people that would cut your throat in a second given the chance, but right now so humble because we were giving them medical treatment and feeding them. You could see in their eyes they hated us as much as they hated the Viet Cong, Viet Mien, Khmer Rough and the North Vietnamese Army. The only difference they could see is we were not taking their youth and making them fight for a cause they were forced to believe in. Truth is you can never force a people to believe in something they do not want to but you can force them to fight for fear of their family being tortured or killed. So we put on our happy faces and proceed to do what we have been told to do.

Even though it was a small village, as the day progressed the people of the village that were awaiting aid began to grow. At first there were maybe ten to fifteen people and by noon after treating them there was fifty or so waiting. They were materializing out of the woods, trees, the rice paddies and where ever else they were coming from, it seemed as though they were actually falling out of the sky. There was mostly the very old or the very young. It appeared as though all the people from thirteen to forty had disappeared possibly sucked up into the Armies of Vietnam either volunteer or otherwise, as long as they had family then they were controllable. Mostly for fear of there family being drug off or killed right in front of them. The draft system employed by the Viet Cong was much different then the system Americans enjoyed. You either went voluntarily or they killed your family while you watched and then they killed you. This of course was to be expected in the valley of death known as Viet Nam.

There was a very thin line between love and hate, dedication and fear. Fear was control, so control led to dedication, how simple the concept! You would never be free as long as you had something left to loose like Janis Joplin said," Freedom was just another word for nothing left to loose!" As long as we have life to loose or the life of a loved one we will never be free, this has been abundantly proven by the way the Khmer Rough and the Viet Cong were able to recruit people to fight for their cause, they would threaten to kill their wives, children, Fathers, Mothers, any and all other relatives and loved ones if they failed to cooperate. Needless to say they not only cooperated, but also became their best soldiers, controlled by fear. Oddly enough, many of the local Vietnamese did not fear losing their life and that was not a very good way to control them, but they did care when it came to losing the lives of their loved ones. They felt that if they were killed they would go to their eternal peace and they would leave this place of on-going suffrage behind.

Life is temporal and expendable and meant very little, after all how precious can something be where there is nothing but pain and suffering and loss is a everyday affair. Kids were constantly being hurt and killed from mines and other types of bombs, legs blown off and arms missing. Life meant nothing, they were well indoctrinated to believe real life would begin when they left this world of pain and suffering.

The more healing the Doctor and Corpsmen did the more people showed up until just about dark, there were more people needing help then had been treated thus far.

Something deep in me clicked, maybe it was the mission of the energy or light source that was leading me to show me this, but I began to believe just maybe this was what the initial intention of the United States involvement in the war effort of the South Vietnamese people, to teach and heal, not to kill and destroy. It was so awesome seeing how Thankful the people were for just getting basic medical care in most cases, this was a completely different analysis of my first thoughts. I had a warmth come over me like a new Father when he sees his new born baby for the first time this was a good thing, the way God intended it to be and I knew at that point I had needed to see and experience this and you could bank on me volunteering for many more of these missions. It would not be difficult to get all of them I wanted, most who went to one never wanted to go back, which I found hard to understand. Maybe it was because it was of a higher calling!

I tried in vain to warn the guards not to get too comfortable and tell them what was going to happen but again no one could or would hear me. That night we stayed there and camped out in the village chief's hut and a couple more designated huts. We were treated like royalty. The next day we were at it again. It seemed like even more folks were in line then even on the day before, where did they come from? Then like every good deed that was done it was met with a negative. About half way through the day, I guess we had become too comfortable, one of the local village kids stole this watch right off one of the Marines hands, it was one of those Seiko watches that you could buy in the Post Exchange for around eight to ten dollars, the Marine started chasing him, after all, the village was secured and sealed, it was considered a safe place, as if there really were any in all of Vietnam by 1970. The Marine started to chase the kid, the lead man told him to let it go but he would not listen, he chased the kid around a corner and through the village to the woods on the other side of the village, that is when we heard the rat, tat, tat, of the AK-47. We ran as fast as we could but it was too late, the Marine guard was dead, and all for a frigging watch that cost him all of eight dollars, but everyone just got too comfortable and forgot the very basic simple rule, never let your guard down never get too comfortable. All within the blink of an eye my attitude changed right back to where it was, and that was the hate of everyone of them, these little bastards were not human, they were frigging animals and total eradication was the only way to deal with them. I would never volunteer for this duty again, after all what good did it do to heal them when next day, they would be busted up, wounded, or killed if they were lucky. I now realized why no one ever volunteered for this duty a second time.

Then the voice of the source leading me came to me and said," imagine you grew up in an environment where just to make it past childbirth was miraculous, and to make it to one year old was shear luck. This meant you just might make it through your preadolescence. Then in all probability as you reach adolescent you will be carted off to become a freedom fighter for the state, the state of communism that is. The best you could hope for then was to live to be very old and useless in the field or that the war will end as that is when your tour of duty will end, when the war is over. " It is easy to blame the child for leading your buddy, your team mate to his death, but then you have to remember the watch was a simple trinket to him, costing all of eight or ten dollars, and to the kid it would be a day he and his family would eat. The trained Marine knew not to take off without his team mates for cover but he got too comfortable and lost sight of where we were and how little they had and what our trinkets and throw −a-ways could purchase for them. After all how many American beer can chi-coms had we seen? Chi-coms are Chinese grenades, home made and deadly most of the time. When it comes to life and death situations it is far easier to see how wrong the other person is and how it is not our fault or that of our teammates. Most of us came from a world where we were rich in comparison to a world of have-nots. Many lived in shacks made of discarded combat ration boxes and dirt floors. Their whole life was about survival, surviving the Vietcong and the North Vietnamese, and then having to survive the Americans. They had never known peace and probably never would. Our world was about moving up the food chain, their world was about surviving the food chain. Even knowing the truth and what is rightfully so it was still hard to focus on the good of these poor folks knowing that you may have just treated them and helped them with their wounds and to rebuild their village and yet they could and would turn on you in the blink of an eye when it came to protecting their family or their own lives. Then would we not do the same given the situation? Was it not relative or subjective? Could I afford sympathy or apathy? This could be like signing ones death warrant when you went on your next patrol in the bush. These were philosophical thoughts for a safer time in life if we made it out of here alive, for now one should only think in the moment and not question what was right and wrong, only what it would take to survive this tour. How little did we expect that the war would follow us home and we would forever have a little piece of our heart in Vietnam, for us, as mainstream society so elaborately puts it, are the lucky ones, we made it back. They still have no idea when they see the news where a Vietnam veteran robs bank, Vietnam veteran kills someone or Vietnam veteran commits suicide, that the war is alive and well and lives on within us forever more! Yeah! We are the lucky ones; free to live with the memories and war for the rest of this life we have here on earth. The resounding question continues do we ever really die and go off to some after world or do we as I said much earlier live a personal hell of repeating over and over again events we can not change and have to watch over and over again the same mistakes and end results from the mistakes. Maybe Heaven is the chance of being recycled, going through the birth cycle all over and growing up again as a different person only the same. Just maybe Heaven is the innocence of our youth!

The Mission

For the most part the mission was a nice set of verbiage put together to make us feel like we were the good boys with the white hats. We were the one's told we were here to stop the counter-insurgency of communist forces in south East Asia. The truth as we knew it at the time, is we were a bunch of innocent youths going off to war to fight for and defend America and our way of life and freedom for all. The real truth was, as I have become to believe, we were going off to war to fight for corrupt corporations that controlled our American government through lobbyists with money to help elect Presidents, congressmen and Senators defending a corrupt government for a people that thought they were fighting for a good cause. How naïve innocence is. Freedom, a word that to this day especially eludes me, and even more since I was forced to develop my education. This forced my eyes open and I had to view things for what they were and not what I was told they are. That meant everything I was taught and had learned to believe in had to be rethought and seen through more critical eyes, those of a fertile mind and a wounded spirit.

Like so many Vietnam veterans we had our belief systems turned upside down. Freedom is the right to live free as long as our living free means doing as our government dictates is social ably acceptable. I am not being cynical, and I still love and believe in my country, but I have been unfortunate enough to have the bubble of my innocence busted, so I have seen the light and the truth and not everything in the big or grown up world is as easy and clear cut as we thought in our youthful innocence. Corruption comes with power and the more power a person or Office has the more corrupt they become. Not always is the masked man going to be on the good side and not all the folks that wear white hats are good or well meaning. Love is conditional and everything, everything on this earth is temporal; nothing will remain the same with exception of greed and death, at least death, as we know it to be, void of our bodily form in the worlds we once lived in with the titles we once had. Just like in combat, get too comfortable and learn too much and the system will find a way to take you out, if not there are enough users that will gladly spread shit about you to help the system work against you and take you down. Everyone has closets filled with garbage and most go unhampered, it is only when you become a threat that your past gets dug up and flaunted for the entire world to see.

Mostly the missions were miserable and boring. You walked all day with enough gear to outfit a large portion of the Viet Cong Army, if there ever was really such a thing. Just maybe in actuality they were something else, demonic or something more sinister, death angels with no mercy. You slept at two-hour intervals changing duty to watch for Charlie or the gooks (the name we gave the Viet Cong), and you dared not to sleep as you were in his world, the enemies back yard, and no matter how good you were, they had been fighting for centuries. The Chinese and French could not defeat them overtly, but the Chinese had done a good job covertly. That is why you would see 250 pound 6 foot tall Vietnamese soldiers in the North Vietnamese Army. These were the ones the News Media would never report to allow America to see the real truth. Instead they would show this big bad Marine holding one gook in each hand and saliva drooling down his chin. Nothing is as it truly is when reported by the bias owners of the news media.

Our mission was supposed to be to collect information on enemy activity in a given area and the size of the units there. Somewhere I was told we were suppose to determine their level of motivation, but that was difficult as it was very difficult to get close enough to them to collect motivational information. It is even more difficult when your level of motivation is very low. We were able to plant monitoring devices along the paths of the enemy and often these were able to gather information until something disabled it such as them being located or blew away on a bombing mission. All the modern technology pales in comparison to experience in the bush and these folks had experience far surpassing our knowledge and experience. When it was hot and dry you had to be careful to stay off the dusty paths not to leave a slight impression that you had been there and it was way too easy to make noise in the dry branches. The human smell of the Americans was more difficult to hide in the heat and dryness, everything from the mosquito spray to the soap we used down to the very food we ate made us smell American The enemy could smell us a mile away and could distinguish whether you washed with lifebuoy or Irish Spring. In the wet you could make a bit more noise and be forgiven, but that meant the enemy could also be closer without you hearing them, it was harder to smell them, and you had to be careful not to leave deep prints in the ground. Either way it was miserable dry season or monsoon season. Each had its own set of advantages and adversities but you grew to accept them and be able to operate accordingly. That is the way a good combat soldier works, every climate and place. Then when you found areas that were saturated with enemy forces, you would call it in and that would be a bombing mission and a feather in some Commanders bonnet. Otherwise you would draw out particular areas of interest and they would later become targets for Naval gunfire, Air or Artillery Units contingent where the targets were located and what was necessary to render the target harmless. After all everyone needed to justify his or her existence and this was the way it would be done.

After the mission was complete we would go to our pick-up area, which was always several clicks away, get picked up and taken back to our unit and be debriefed (using the term lightly). We would then have a steak and the club would open where we would get drop down commode hugging drunk so we could pass out and sleep. Of course sleep would not last long and after a while no matter how drunk you got it did not matter, you would still toss and turn and see people and things that were not actually there. You were forever changed and would be among the walking dead for the remainder of your life.

Valley of the Dolls

gain I was somehow transported to another area. At first I did not recognize anyone it was dark and the fog stood about two feet off the ground, it was like a sequel to Dark Shadows, and one expected the ware wolves and vampires to start coming out, and they were there Just in a different form then what we see in the books, they often wore black pajamas. As I looked closer, I noticed the American soldiers were lying quietly on the ground waiting, waiting for what? Maybe death, maybe first light and then they would move out, strange how by day the enemy was Farmers with no way to distinguish them and Viet Cong by night. This took the citizen soldier to a whole new level. Then we are asked why we killed or maimed civilians. You would see them in the rice paddies and fields and swear you had seen them stalking you that previous night in the bush. Then again after a few months fighting them, they all began to look alike, a man with a gun of Asian decent, intent on killing you, this made it more personal.

You could see that there was a vague outline of a village just ahead, was it friendly or would we start receiving incoming as soon as we neared it, you never knew what to expect. It was just a few more minutes before the sun would rise and the day would begin, the troops all huddled

141

up together and the orders were given, they all said a prayer that went something like this," Lord if you should will this not our day to die then see it fit to watch the backs of the rest of the team. If you choose this to be our day then Please let me go out fighting and be killed instantly and not left behind to have my body mutilated. As we drew closer to the village our eyes opened up and there were Vietnamese Villagers ran through with long logs and hung there to die on these logs like a version of the crucifix where the path was lined with dying human beings on posts. We knew this would not be a good day; it already started off with a horrific view that sadly enough had become commonplace. As we arrived in the village there was no one there, they were all dead, at least that seemed to be the case when this old man come running out completely naked and trying to speak, waiving his arms frantically, we would learn he had no tongue, it had been cut out so he could not talk. After being in combat for a while, you either get savvy, a sort of sixth sense or you die young, this is where the experience comes into play, We knew we had to get out of here and fast as we could, you somehow just knew this was an ambush and we were already halfway into it. God! Which way should we turn, I tried to tell them, I tried to warn them but they could not hear me. We sent the old man ahead of us like chumming for salmon, and when the enemy fire broke out we knew the Viet Cong was there, because had it been North Vietnamese Soldiers, they would have waited until we were all in the middle and we would be like shooting ducks in a circus.

Somehow everyone survived this ambush and the enemy rapidly departed, at least those survived, only to live to fight another battle on another day.

As for the villagers, we went back and dug holes to properly bury them and then called it in and started towards our pick-up area on peak alert just knowing at any time we would get hit again.

The Ammo Dump And Eod

A gain I was some how transported by this light or energy source to another area where I was in a enclosed area and there was a small contingency of guards, a couple of EOD personnel and some maintenance people but nothing else, and the entire area was barren. There were very large bunkers under ground and in them were all kinds of fragmentation devices and ordinances. There were ordinances of every imaginable type and some I never imagined. The men there were placed there for one reason, and that was to guard the ammo bunkers. It was really not bad duty, just boring as hell. All day long they would walk the perimeter and some would be strategically placed at the bunkers of major interest. Then every four hours they would change watch (guards). Fortunately there were books there, possibly left by previous crews that drew this wonderful duty, and yes I am being somewhat cynical. Books were read that I am sure I would never have read and probably would not have, had boredom not began to manifest itself in evil ways, like forcing folks to exercise and the like. There was a small mess hall, and it was set up for the maintenance crews and guards so the hours varied. It was not bad; at least it was not C-Rations, after a while it seems as though you were gong to live on C-Rations and it

144

was always the luck of the draw. I loved the ham and eggs; it came with crackers, cheese and a chocolate bar and was really filling. You add some Tabasco sauce, melt the cheese and eat with the crackers and it was somewhat palatable. Instead there were lots of hamburgers, hotdogs and the like since it was easy to deliver, and easier to prepare, we always had potatoes; the military had perfected the art of preparation when it came to potatoes. The cooks could easily prepare them a hundred different ways. About eighty of them involved mashing of course and needless to say someone had to peel the potatoes. The rest were fried, baked, and boiled. The military cook is an innovative person, they get bored and God only knows what will come out of it. I can remember the deep -fried Vietnamese potatoes. The potatoes were carved out salted and peppered, battered and deep - fried paying special attention not to damage the carving. This was then served with what the troops all called," red death", blood red, greasy corned beef brisket right out of the can and boiled. I always thought it was really good but most of the troops hated it and placed it right up there with liver and onions, which I also liked. It did however have a tendency to give you a serious case of acid indigestion, but the Corpsman had a cure for that.

After a couple of boring weeks, things began to change, just to add a bit of excitement I would guess and keep everyone on their toes. At night just around eleven the rockets would start flying in. It was not a real big deal as long as one of the ammo containers did not take a direct hit. If it did all hell would break loose, as there was enough explosives and ordinances that it would have taken out the entire area both inside and outside the perimeter not to mention the personnel and in all probability the next village over which was a little over a mile away.

The ammunition and explosives used by the Viet Cong was not always the best and on occasion it would not explode right away. There were Chinese grenades lying around the perimeter made from a diversity of cans, spam cans, beer cans and the like, a return of the littered cans the Americans left behind or riddled around the area. There were rockets that would be buried head first in the compound and you never knew if they would explode on impact, and when it does not explode it possibly will if it is pulled out of the ground or it may explode at anytime without notice, this is when EOD does their thing and why they were there with us. Engineer Ordinance Disposal Technicians were crazy as bed bugs and many missing fingers, most of them alcoholics and for obvious reasons. I watched the EOD personnel tie a rope to the rockets and attach it to the jeep and just pull it out of the ground to what they deemed a safe area before they worked on it. They were really good at what they did and in order to do what they did they had to be crazy. As time would pass I would learn they were both very knowledgeable and crazy. I had seen them do the procedure of tying off a rocket and pulling it to a safe zone and then disarming it on many occasions, but one day it was pouring down and they hastily yanked the rocket out of the ground, went to pull it to a safe zone when all hell broke loose, the explosion rocked the entire camp and all you could see was metal and flesh combined flying through the air in almost a psychedelic kaleidoscope. It was beautiful and horrible at the same time it made you feel like you must have somehow dropped acid and was having this surreal experience or really bad trip. Then the reality hit home that this was two men, two human beings, fathers, husbands, sons and friends that were reduced to hamburger and metal shards, this occurred in an area called Tuy Duc in a little known ammunition dump. To this day I am not sure if we were in Cambodia or not and as a young trooper could really have cared less since it was just another place I had not heard about when I was young just like Vietnam and Laos. To me it was all the same, poorly ran countries and all commies! That is why it did not matter in the least to me; after all we were here to stop the communists were we not? Communists were communists in the eyes of a young man from Kentucky or any other small city in good old America USA, we were taught, or should I say indoctrinated to believe this from small kid days. This being somewhere between 1969 and 1970, it would not be too many years until the illustrious Khmer Rough made the grandiose attempt to commit genocide of the Cambodian people, just like the Communists had pretty much accomplished with the true Vietnamese peoples.

What was pathetic is you could talk to a man over breakfast about where he was from in the real world, talk about his family and how his children were doing and then the next hour or less you were watching him become pieces of flesh and meat mixed with shards of metal. Worse yet you had come to accept this as the normal. Had we become so cynical and callous that it just did not matter anymore or were we in some way trying to protect our sanity and not deal with the reality of what had just occurred? What had happened to these youths of America, had they so drastically changed and more serious yet, could they ever come back even after leaving this God forsaken world in the Far East! Where did the youth of the young men go, where did the youth of all of us go? Had we been robbed of our youth for a war we were destined to loose, prevented from winning because of the politics? There should never be news reporters on the battle front with the combat soldiers, war is hell and that is all there is, when reduced to survival mode and animalistic behaviorisms then atrocities happen, and what ever it takes to get the information needed is the way it will always go, Look at the way the Japanese, Koreans, Nazis, and Vietnamese treated us as Prisoner Of War's, then ask if you think we treated them worse or even as bad. There will never be any good come from war, and when war ends, there is always another waiting or started before the other one ends. We are merely a nation of war in a world of wars. Sadly enough nothing good ever comes of war and the collateral damage is phenomenal, the death of innocent women and children. As long as there is war, innocent people will die and there is nothing proper or nice about it.

DownTime

The worse time in a war for the warrior is the down time, this is the time where you are in the so-called," rear with the beer". This is a time where you get your gear replaced or repaired. You are in a fairly well protected area, and only the rockets to contend with and they were infrequent and not well directed. In the mean time you had three hot's and cot and plenty of almost cold beer to drink. You could even get a shower. This is the time you were to rest up and be refreshed for the next operation. The problem is this was also the time you would have to think, think about where you were, what you were doing and had done. You were not in that constant state of awareness that prevented you from thinking about anything except what was ahead or where your team was and what was at the next turn.

Your thoughts went to your girl back home, your wife or someone else's wife. It was mom and pop, and what was going on back home. There were your friends, if you had any, and what you would be doing if you were back home. For most of those I was with, this was the time we bullshit ourselves as we really had no idea what we would be doing back home, because we really had no back home, as a close knit family would know it.

For the most of us we were trained to be cannon fodder

from the time we were born till right here and now. This was
not an outward and obvious programming, but a very effective
one. We grew up seeking somewhere to fit in, something we
could be good at and accepted. We were trained in the way
we were raised; the caste we grew up in, even though we
claim there is no caste in America. The long lonely nights we
spent seeking something that would make us feel important
or wanted or needed. Constantly in trouble at school and
just barely on the right side of the law falling over the fence
from time to time. Many of us were living in foster homes
and never owning anything and constantly having to watch
our backs. For the most part we learned to survive and how
to do it well, where to find the next meal, a good set of
clothing that we would steal or gamble for and if given the
chance work for. If we needed a shoulder to lean on if only
for a few minutes at a time we would find it, and that is the
extent of what we knew love to be.

Then there were the questions of why we are here to
start with and what we were accomplishing by being here.
We go to a village and the Viet Cong would kill all the
people and destroy the village, if we went in and the Viet
Cong was there or had recently been there and the village
was not destroyed we would kill all the people and destroy
the village, what sense did it make and what did it matter
anyhow? The people were just as dead no matter what the
cause was, what good is a cause anyhow if you are dead,
how then can you appreciate it.

Then came the question, " What the hell was this war
about anyhow"? Why do I hate the person I am trying to
kill when I have never met him or her and they hate me so
much they too are trying to kill me? Is it we hate each other
or is it because our governments tell us we should hate each

other? When you think about it they are only doing what you are, fighting for what they think is right or in the case of many to protect their families. Some were even fighting because they were taken and told if they did not fight for the cause they would be considered as an enemy of the state or government and their families would be killed in front of them. Some love of country this instills in the common soldier, I wonder how I would feel and most Americans if we were forced to fight for this reason or in this way!

Of course this is the time the Marine Corps as I am sure the other branches do, puts you on guard duty so your mind does not tear you down. You have training, the Marine Corps likes there training, but like they say the more you sweat in training the less you bleed in combat. We were all about letting the enemy give his life for his country instead of us giving our lives for our country. As much as I hate to admit it, there was a good reason for what I felt was madness, it kept our heads together and made us focus on something other then the why's and what if's. Our minds when left dormant will kill us if we allow it to. I have known many good men who have fallen because they allowed their mind to wander and failed to focus leading them to be caught off guard. A mind is a terrible thing to waste but a dangerous place to attempt to live. It did not take too long until you were ready to get back in the bush and away from all the bullshit in the rear with all the brass covering their ass and trying to look good. It amazes me that their were sixteen Generals killed in the Vietnam war, the part that is most amazing is you just did not see Generals in Vietnam especially in the bush. If you did see them you had to get all pretty and look like you were a garrison Marine and then they left and it was business as usual.

A Shau Valley

omehow I was lifted to, or lead to this area that did not seem familiar to me, but it well should have. If I am not mistaking, this is where 1st Battalion 9th Marines earned its title of the walking dead.

It was a nasty, wet and cold day, it seemed like the rain was completely saturating our uniforms and through to our bones. It actually hurt to even walk because the joints of every part of our bodies ached like arthritis in old men. Our mission was to set up anti personnel mines as boobie traps along the trails leading to the mountain. This was the old sight of Operation Dewey Canyon and Operation Apache. There was the great battle for the real estate up the AP BIA Mountain in January of 1969 where countless Marines from 9th Marines lost their lives. It was a strong hold and area of operation for the North Vietnamese Army the North's finest, those six-foot plus 250-pound Chinese mainstream America never seemed to hear about. This would become known as the Hamburger Hill for obvious reasons. This was 1970 over a year after that heartbreaking loss of so many men and it was thought the strong hold had been broken, but the enemy was extremely resilient, and there was very heavy influx of NVA soldiers in the area, thought to be another buildup of troops and equipment.

No one really understood why we were here, just the same answer as always, to gather information, but then, if that was why we were there, why were we planting and hiding anti personnel mines along the trails leading up to the mountain? All I could hope for as an outside spirit if you will, is that they were not going to hit the shit again like they had the year before, I thought this was neutralized, but the signs around the area and the obvious lack of concern to show activity was saying something entirely different. You just got that sick feeling in the pit of your stomach of impending doom. You just instinctly knew something was seriously wrong and that was a bad feeling, keeping you with borderline nausea and these cold sweats that would not stop, you could not only feel it but somehow you could taste the bile that kept rising as you continued to work. You could hear voices and hear noises of movement, but throughout the day you never seen anyone passing or leaving. You could tell by the amount of movement that they somehow had to be coming and going throughout the day and night. There were no footprints to follow, and no units passing you. It was like they were ghosts passing through and around you and you never seeing them. Granted the jungle canopy was thick but you would think you would have to see at least a small contingency of soldiers. Whatever it was must be big and we would have to find out so we could get the word back to our intelligence personnel, the S-2 section so they could brief the General who would in turn formulate his own battle plan according to the intelligence information he had and what it looked like to him was going on, and what it appeared it would take to inflict heavy casualties that would be instrumental to win the attack on whichever enemy it was at that particular time in that given area. This tour for Officers was a very big career developer and they would rotate in and out every six months, so the facts must report heavy body counts inflicted with overwhelming odds and the accomplishment of the mission at great pain and suffering, but of course with good leadership skills by the particular Officer. It was never about winning the war, just what they could get from the war. They never started it, but they may as well get what they could from it since they had to be there anyhow and the reality that incoming rockets could kill them or sappers could get lucky, did exist. They needed this show of bravery by bloodshed to develop in their art or trade as a combat Officer.

We continued to place anti-personnel mines in strategic locations and then we got the word to work our way up the mountain to gather whatever information we could. This was to prove to be a truly arduous task, just getting up the hill with the pouring down rain and the mud. IT seemed absolutely impossible for this to provide a positive outcome, as cover and concealment was hard if not impossible in this thick blanket of forest going up the mountain slipping and sliding in the mud and wet rocks. We sounded like a tank with all the noise made from breaking branches and the like. The quieter we tried to be the louder it seemed we were. This may have just been us thinking we were making an inordinate amount of noise since we had become quite adept at keeping quite, like the slogan, swift, silent and deadly, our motto for Recon. Most of the time you could tell the enemy was coming or was there when all the critters stopped making their noise. No crickets, birds, etc... a sure sign something horrible was about to happen. Total quietness was one of the scariest things in the world. Just like the Pavlov Ian dogs, the quiet was our stimulus and when we got hit we returned well-directed fire to inflict heavy enemy losses as a response. We slowly etched our way to the peak of the mountain, painfully slow and trying at every movement to a point where you just knew you could not take another step. There were massive snakes to contend with as well, but we could not let this stop our endeavor, we were on a mission and if you learn nothing else about the Marines you knew the mission must be completed no matter what the losses. You could not be sure if the enemy would find you first or if Mother Nature's pets would get you. We would accomplish our mission and we hoped we would get out alive to tell about it, there was no retreat, it was up or down and either way would be nasty in a hurry. Most of us only had a few months left and had already started to fill out our short timer calendars and this in no way gave a comforting feeling of sliding through the next ninety days without threat of serious bodily injury or possibly death. This was starting to appear like a suicide mission, another way of eliminating the lower caste of America's society, the Grunt! In time of war all Americans love him and in Peace he is a burden to society as he gave all he had! He is now crippled or psychologically impaired, a burden to society.

First we have to survive to get to the place where we can become a burden, right here and now we need to survive, and survival is a challenge at best!

Up we continue to climb and it seems more of a challenge as we climb, crazy as it sounds the lyrics of stairway to heaven come rushing through my mind, a song by Led Zeppelin; "There's a feeling I get, when I look to the west, and my spirit is crying for leaving, in my thoughts, I have seen, rings of smoke through the trees, and the voices of those who stand looking, and it's whispered that soon, if we all call the tune, then the piper will lead us to reason, and a new day will dawn, for those who stand long, and the forest will echo with laughter, yes there's two paths you can go, but in the long run, there's still time to change, the road you are on". Will the next step be the end? We will continue upwards until we have reached the very peak of the mountain, more voices and noises of equipment clanging and rattling. We are almost there and as we arrive, we see what we did not want to see; soldiers everywhere and we would be seen if we dared to get closer. We begin our rapid decent, we need to get far enough down to report the activity and call in air power to clear the area. There should be an artillery base camp close enough to finish off the job. We need to get farther down so we can call it in and not be victims of our own fire mission. Finally days pass and we are clear. It seems like weeks, but at least we are now clear to call it in and watch the fireworks. It is amazing how we were never observed; maybe they were just so confident and secure that they did not feel there was anything to be concerned with. Overconfidence and getting too comfortable is deadly, just as deadly as fear.

The mission is called in and then the fourth of July type fireworks from high and low, it is a beautiful sight and yet it devastation and killing. Maybe this is the light; at least it will be the last light many of the enemy on the hill will see. What makes him my enemy is because he is on the other side and his government has convinced him as mine has me that we are right and all others are wrong, besides he wants to kill me. I am the good guy, and what makes it so, I am still alive and he is not, that in itself is all the validation I need at this point of survival. The thought that we are in his country and on his turf intruding in a civil war, but we were invited!

A Dance of Life

I am again lifted by this energy source and out of the area to another area and operation to observe more while in the spirit somewhere between dream world and reality.

I found myself down at a flood- wall somewhere in Danang; there the children were fishing, no special rods and reels, not even a bamboo pole. They would throw a string with a bait on it into the water and when a fish would bite, they would jerk the line and pull it in, the fish were not large, but enough and a good meal would be had by all. As I watched I almost forgot where I was, just a bunch of kids fishing and frolicking for the day. It was good to hear the laughter and see them working together for the good of all, even making a game of it. It amazed me that children can have fun even in this God forsaken place, a place where death was always present and waiting just around the corner, and back home our children and even adults are totally devastated when the television is on the blink or the electricity goes out temporarily, they had neither.

My mind started to wander back to my youth, back to the days when we would swim and fish in the Ohio River. A time when we would camp out for fun, build a small fire and cook out, sometimes fishing all night or singing around the camp fire roasting marshmallows and hotdogs on a stick or piece of wire. We had no fear, no adult supervision, and the only thing we had to fear was a snake, but we had our rifles and the law was fine with that, we were only fourteen, fifteen and sixteen years old. We never registered our guns; they were tools for hunting to kill for food and for protection from the wild animals, or for fun to go target shooting. There was no need for a fishing license to fish in the river or hunting license to go on some ones farm and kill squirrels, rabbits and deer. Hell most of the farmers appreciated it since these were pests to the farmer, eating his crops and seeds. No hunting or fishing license period until you turned sixteen. Where did things go so wrong, when did all these restrictions and controls take place? I never picked up a gun in anger or to use against another human being until our government told me to! If you had a beef you went to fist-a-cuffs, and that was only if you could not talk it out. It seems as though we never really had a problem with guns until the government told us they were evil. Now we have robberies almost daily, shootings and the likes. Strange how this was not the case until our government decided to have gun control and registration.

Then at seventeen everything changed, I joined the Marine Corps thinking it would help me and allow me to make something out of myself while serving my country. They placed a rifle in my hands and taught me to hunt people and kill them not for sustenance but because they were the enemy, what made them the enemy? Our government said so and that was all I needed to know, I was a Marine, my life was dedicated to killing, It was beaten in my head from sun-up to sun-down twenty-four seven. Kill! Kill! Kill! Was the ongoing chant? The better I became at it the more accolades I got and the better my chance of making it back home. The problem comes when you, as did I start to enjoy having the power over another human being to take their life and having no remorse over it. When and if I can survive and go home I have to register my guns and get a hunting and fishing license. I honestly believe we need less government and laws and more power to the people.

Now here I was in a country I had never heard of as a child, a place called Vietnam! Where the hell did all these strange countries come from? Vietnam, Thailand, Cambodia, Laos, and Burma! Not only did the places sound strange, but also what the hell did it matter what went on over here so far away from our home. Here I was, doing what I never dreamed of in a country I never heard of for a reason that made no sense to me. Fighting to stop the counterinsurgency of communist forces in Southeast Asia. What the hell does all that jargon mean? From my meaningless viewpoint it meant to come over here, kill everyone I could, cause as much hate and discontent as possible destroying everything along my pathway, make the people dependant on us, then leave them hanging in the end, to fall prey to the very people we were trying to eradicate. Meanwhile the Khmer Rough was trying to commit genocide on the Cambodians and we were as surely allowing and participating in the genocide of the Vietnamese people.

And the lyrics of another song come racing through my mind, I can't remember the song but the lyrics were, "that's me in the corner loosing my religion, there I've said it again". Everything I was taught to believe was now a mixture of confusion, fear, hate, frustration, and doubt.

I could vaguely remember a time when things were less confusing and freedom was a real thing as far as I knew in my little corner of the world, in my protected environment, protected from war, famine, and government controls, at least I thought it was that way. Money was not a big thing as barter was alive and functioning well, the Doctor would come to your house and sometimes he was paid in fish or corn or whatever you were growing or had on hand. The local mechanic was you, your cousin, uncle or dad, a twelve pack of beer in the cooler, under a shade tree. The family garden was a vital part of the household and provided all the fresh vegetables the family needed and wanted. You could pick a tomato off the vine and eat it without having to worry about the insecticides and contamination. We would put fresh cow manure on the garden, and dig it into the soil, never worrying about E coli, where did it all go wrong? Did I fall asleep and everything changed while I was in some form of comma? What happened to Sundays at Grand Mothers house, where we would always be in for a feast, the whole family would pull together, and it was turtle soup, or fried squirrel, rabbit, venison, fish or grandma's special fried chicken, and always fresh apple, cherry or rhubarb pie!

Well, Mother ran away with some other guy, dad divorced her, grandma got old, the family fell apart, and here I was sitting my ass in some foreign country fighting for some cause that I did not understand, hoping to live long enough to get back to the country that I no longer knew, that had turned upside down while I was away, or then again, maybe I was just seeing it through different eyes. I left just three short years earlier, and now I did not even recognize home, long hair on the guys, gun controls on the people, kids could not carry pocket knives to school, drugs I never heard of before now popular and everyone going on trips and their cars never leaving the driveway. Music changed dramatically and I was lost. Glue tubes for putting together model cars; a passion of my youth, now restricted purchases since people were getting high on it. The river I fished and swam in as a youth was contaminated and warnings against swimming in it or eating the fish. People talking about Love and Peace while riots and radical demonstrations going on and cities burning. On the television every night were body counts, and a group of Vietnam veterans against the war demonstrating, a guy named Kerry throwing back his medals he claimed he earned in Vietnam and a actress named Jane Fonda laughing and carrying on with North Vietnamese soldiers saying how the war was wrong and we should not be there causing the prisoners of war to be tortured even more mercilessly.

Where the hell was I? Had I dropped off the face of the earth and fell into some unknown black hole watching the world I knew destroying itself?

For now all I had to do was get out of the place I was in, prepare for another operation/mission, another battle, another firefight and hopefully another day of surviving. Nothing would ever be the same again, for me, and many of the other veterans I knew!

Time To Move Out!

ime to focus, another mission, the war waits for nothing or no one and especially a non-rate. The Viet Cong await us! More people to kill and more to die, Uh RAH!!!

Here I go again, to another place another situation, another part of my living hell between dream world and reality where all I can do is watch and can not change the outcome no matter how hard I try, as the past is in the past and all we can do is accept what it is and try to move forward. The mind is a funny thing, it will not allow us to forget what was and replays it in vivid color when we least expect it, releasing the demons of the past in full force. In our efforts to kill them we give them strength, so we must embrace them and attempt to put them at rest.

I find myself again in the Arizona area, why are we here, we have combed almost every inch of this area on as many occasions. There must be something going on because the S-2 in their infinite wisdom would not just send us here for no reason, maybe a troop build-up or something like it or maybe to inflict misery and justify our existence by keeping us humping. I was just a peon following orders. Holy shit! The grass around hill 200 is smashed down and there is an anti- aircraft gun on top of the hill, when did they place that there? God these bastards are good! Again the quiet, it is just way too quiet, too many signs of recent movement. There is the feeling you are being watched, you know it, and somehow because of your sixth sense you just feel eyes on you and your movement.

Again I tried to warn them and no one could hear me, the sky is now filled with small arms fire, thick with lead, this will be the end for many of us, correction, them as I am not really here in the living or even dead for all I know. I can hear the run on fire of a machine gun, the rat! Tat! Tat! Of an Ak-47, shit has hit the fan, we are up the proverbial creek with no paddle, we need to some how jump off the boat and swim clear, meaning get the hell out of Dodge! I look around and one after another Marine falls victim to the barrage of fire, the corpsman can only help so many. Call in artillery; call in Air strikes, for Christ sakes call something in before it is all over, damn! One of the Corpsmen went down, now only one to do all the healing work.

All the sudden a bomb comes flying in and sounds like a train flying overhead, it lands solid and takes out the anti-aircraft gun, the enemy soldiers in the field start to turn to head toward the emplacement to protect their command post, we are finally the chasers instead of being chased. Our chase is very slow as we have lost so many of the platoon, our forty two man platoon is almost rendered useless as we have so many down and so many to carry the downed Marines, best find a way out while we have what we have left. It takes two men to carry one, so if fourteen are down that is the whole platoon! Two to carry and one down, three each times fourteen is 42 the entire platoon! No one to complete the mission until the medivac birds arrive and carry off the wounded, then we will have 28 men to complete the mission of the 42, and we were shorthanded at that. We must make the enemy think we are stronger then we are, make them think we have more people and firepower then we do, at least until the medical evacuation birds leave. This is the only way we will survive; if they knew how weak we were then they would surely come down for a mop up operation taking all of us out. Finally the helicopters start to arrive; first they circle the hill to get a bomb damage analysis and then pick our men. Their circle for BDA only took in a few small arms fire. Load up the wounded and dead then off to mop up the position, take no prisoners we are told, as if we had planned on it anyhow! Escorting enemy takes way too much energy and manpower and we had none to spare. We were the few, the proud, but why always too few to do the mission when we read in the stars and strips how many troops are in Vietnam, where the hell are they? Definitely not here, in the bush with us, where we need them, economy of forces? Whose economics are we working with, some college graduate at the Pentagon who never spent a day in real combat! I could already imagine, some Captain or Major is sitting back in the rear with the beer bragging about how many confirmed kills he has, while the inordinate amount of wounded lay in the hospital. Then what does it really matter, it will continue as long as some officer thinks he will get promoted based on a body count that is at best exaggerated. Off we go, not only in harms way, but harm making a way! Our mission to eradicate every single living being in the area, and after that barrage of fire and our dead and wounded we were primed and ready to take care of business. Fear is a funny thing, it can turn to hate without a moments notice.

As we continue on our mission, we know there is a

good probability that many more will be wounded or killed as we will inevitably run into small pockets of the enemy and we have no idea where they may be or what type of cover they have, they are in fact the masters of concealment, having lived in the bush most if not their whole lives. We must also remember we are on their turf, in their back yard, and they know it well! Somewhere in my now sick mind something clicks and I feel like I am on a rabbit hunt and the only difference is they are two legged, shoot back, and are useless for eating. God how sick! But thoughts are thoughts and they make the unreal come to life and this was my life so we were rabbit hunting as far as my mind would correlate things.

This was another one of those lucky missions, we did hit a few pockets, but they were taken out relatively fast with grenades, and only one of our men was wounded, but he would be okay until we completed the mission and could carry him back with us. That was his desire to complete the mission, as would be any good Marine. The Corpsman felt it would be fine to allow him this request mission. For us Marines it was very important to complete the mission even if it meant certain death.

Finally we had completely swept the area and it was clear, so for added proof, much of the area was fired up with napalm, if there was anything alive it would take care of that.

I Thought I Had Seen It All!

As I came to the realization of where I had been somehow transported for this next mission I found myself in this helicopter. I had seen it before in another life as a young Marine but I still felt like my heart stopped. We were again operating with the South Korean Marines. South Korean Marines have a way of gathering information we could not seem to acquire. Their ways may seem crude, but in war there are occasions when drastic measures must be taken. I watched as this Korean Marine Interrogator decided he was getting nowhere with conventional interrogation so as I watched as he threw this Vietnamese man out the hell hole (opening in the bottom of the helicopter), the Vietnamese man began to spout off all kinds of things, I do not know if they were profanities or he was saying prayers, but he was definitely on a short route to his death, then he looked at the other and said something in Vietnamese, and when I looked at the Vietnamese man, I could read it all over him, he was scared to death and knew he was looking at certain death. He was trying to tell the South Korean in his Vietnamese and broken English that the Korean Marine had just screwed up and threw the man who actually had the information from the helicopter to his death, but if he wanted, he would make something up.

This is how it sounded to me. As the Korean Marine went to him, he started running off like a stereo on a speed too fast for the record album. Information gathered, the Korean Marine had accomplished his mission, and the Vietnamese man was now useless, so he threw him out to his definite death as well. Using the information gathered, the Korean wanted us dropped off at a location he told the pilot, we were told to work with them and the Commander was our senior. We went as we were told, and after we landed and disembarked, we were standing in the middle of nowhere with nothing or no one around, or were they! Sure enough the Korean Marine had found catchments of arms. It seemed a bit odd that only two or three soldiers were guarding it so the Korean decided he would find out the truth, he had one of his men ask a question and everytime he felt the answer was wrong, he would cut the soldier with his k-bar, deep enough to hurt badly and bleed good but not deep enough to kill him, this could last all night. By the time the Korean Marine got his information, the Vietnamese must have been cut a hundred times and I mean really cut deep. The man was barely alive, so the Korean tied him to the ground after stripping him and allowing the blood to run freely, and left him to die and be eaten by the animals. We called in the guns and the Airforce accommodated us in a flying barrage of firepower that totally decimated the area. It was a dark black burning ember when we left, not a tree, a plant, or even a piece of scrub grass was left.

I had heard on several occasions that information gathered through torture was generally unreliable. I also seen much of the information gathered be useful and saved many a Marines life.

The Fireman

As rapidly as I arrived I was again transported to another place where there was yet another atrocity I would experience. I felt like I was somehow in a trance or something and I did not want to see any more, but against my will I was in another situation in this dream world that seemed so real. There was a Vietnamese man that took off running as we approached the rice paddy, why we had no idea, but he seemingly had something big to hide and we were about to find out what it was.

When people loose sight of what the mission really is, have too much time and experience dealing with death, dying and killing, things happen and they become like a pack of wild dogs, and this was one of those cases through and through. There is no control over these wild dogs, they have a mind of their own and generally blood thirsty.

First off the Vietnamese man was captured after being taken down by the dog, he was badly bite and bleeding. He was then tied to a tree and questioned as he bled, he refused to answer any questions as far as we could tell, and in all actuality he probably could not speak English well enough to tell us if he knew anything. The team was worked up into a wild craze, like a bunch of sharks in a feeding frenzy, nothing the man could say or could have said would have mattered; he was going to be tortured to death. It all starts out to be a means of rapid take over and they would not be given the chance to run, you too must accept this is all part of the cycle of life, I could only hope and pray there is an eternal place called heaven. The mans feet were tied up, then he was tied to a tree upside down, then to my surprise, a fire was built under the mans head, then he was slowly lowered to within inches and more fuel was placed on the fire until it was lapping at the top of his head, all I could do was pray he would die very soon as the team was getting a thrill watching the man suffer as his brain fried and he finally would die a very painful death. It was way too slow for my liking as they would lift him periodically to ensure he did not burn too rapidly so he could get the full benefit of the suffering.

Finally by the grace of God the man died, I was sickened just watching, but no one else seemed bothered and it was never mentioned in any reports, just another of the faceless, and nameless gooks! I could not help but come to the realization that we had become them, we were just as evil and bitter as they or maybe more so, they did it to accomplish something, get information, we did it for fun, and that made it sick and evil in a deep, sick, disturbing kind of way. How had we digressed to such a level? I was innocent, some may say, but we stood and watched if we did not actually participate. That made us just as guilty and it would be with us for all eternity, dreams would filter in during their sleep and it would never go away, a human being tortured to death just for shits and grins. Maybe this was the payment I was giving back, the constant revisiting of these atrocities where the results would always be the same and we could not change the event or the outcome.

Who were we? How did we get to where we are? Had we crossed into the gates of an eternal hell? But we are the good guys, Sure thing! Who were we fooling? Had we become so blind we could not see the difference between good and evil, right and wrong? What is right? What is wrong when you merely survive in this land God forgot or turned a blind eye to, this Hell on earth?

It is scary how we can justify the horrific torture of a human being and have no remorse about it. Of course to have remorse we have to feel we have done something wrong and after we live or co-exist in an environment like this where death lives with us daily and from minute to minute we loose contact with the reality of what is right and what is wrong. The end results justify the means no matter how profoundly evil it may seem to the outside world, shit happens and we move on, otherwise we wallow in it and ultimately we will drown in our own shit.

When we get to the edge the only thing that keeps us from going over is shear balance. Balance in this situation is seeing the right and good in all the evil and wrong. We must stay balanced and centered even if it is a lie just to justify our actions. If we can convince ourselves of our own bullshit then we will remain centered and balanced, other wise we will fall over. That means walking with our personal demons for all time.

Again I was somehow directed or led away from this scene and to yet another atrocity. When, if, or where the atrocities occurred I do not know, all I know is I was for some unexplained reason forced to see these occurrences, atrocities up close and personal, was I the perpetrator or was I part of it with others?

I could not even begin to envision I would or could

have participated in any of these atrocities. Maybe it was only in my mind in this dream world. I was walking in this dream world just outside the realm of reality. I was being forced to see what mankind is actually capable of given full range and without law or direction of good leadership. But then again it was a long time ago and in another life and at the time another world.

Did God still Love me? I have been told his love was unconditional, but surely unconditional love can be pushed to the limits. Was I still considered his child? Was I disowned as I have seen so many earthly parents do to their children? Maybe I was merely a bastard child, or worse yet was I now a child of Satan himself! Just maybe all this viewing was Satan escorting me and showing me how I had earned my status as his adopted child. If that were the case then I was right, I was living my personal hell, somewhere between dream world and reality in the spirit world of life here on earth. Then maybe this was the message, I was now dead and I was traveling in my new life or death, had they become one, with the union called hell?

Maybe I would never again awaken to see the smiles of those I had loved, or hear their laughter. Just maybe I had learned on a large scale that what I was told about man being inherently evil was true. I had now seen evil at its prime and I would never be the same again! I was a damaged goods. But I was not alone, as I would later in life learn; there is a multitude of us who now suffer from the affects of Post Traumatic Stress Disorder. PTSD was like cancer, left alone it would completely encompass the body and destroy us, but properly treated we could put it in remission until another trauma occurred in life to take us over the edge.

City of Death

ere I was in another place not knowing when, or how I arrived, I was just there. The City itself was reminiscent of an old western town with Asian influence. There were the basic General store, the medical clinic, a restaurant, local bar and Temple. Dogs ran the streets that seemed too skinny and half fed sniffing in every garbage pile. The roads were all dirt with dust flying everywhere and mud slides when it rained. There were very few vehicles, mostly bikes and scooters. Strangely enough the war efforts had managed to work itself here in this village, there were many American products, soap powder, chocolate and cassette tapes. Behind the wood frame semi-western style houses, Semi-western style since there was no indoor plumbing and had community outhouses and kitchen, was the c-ration card- board box houses. The people were poor, especially since the war had always existed to them, which caused the communists to take most all the items they had that were useful to the war effort. The Vietnamese were a practical bunch and they could make the most insignificant item useful. The c-ration boxes were coated with some form of wax material so the rain would not penetrate them; they filled them with sand or dirt and stacked them using a mud type mortar. This actually made

172

for a very strong and comfortable house. They still had dirt floors and thatch roofs, but it was all they needed. They did not need a kitchen as they all cooked outside in a form of community kitchen. I could not help but wonder what they would do for monsoon season with all the rain, surely they were somehow prepared for that, after all they had lived here long before me and with some luck long after me. Around the village and behind almost every house was a family garden and rice paddies everywhere. One could actually imagine it could be a peaceful life if the war would leave them alone, but as with most villages, they would build and rebuild and continue on with life.

It had to be somewhere around ten in the morning as the sun was up in full force without a breeze anywhere. There were smells of garlic, onions, peppers and fermented fish sauce; it was not my favorite smell with the fish sauce. The people continued to scurry around as though they could not see us, they had their daily world to live and they would continue to do it until they were killed or wounded so bad they could not. These people were hardcore, I have actually seen Vietnamese women give birth and go right back to work. You could hate the people but you would definitely have to respect their tenacity. In a situation like this one, you had to make sure you did not get too loose observing and letting your mind wander, you never knew what the village may hold in store for you. The sad reality is whatever waits in the dark is probably not good for you or your teammates.

Stop, look, and listen, that is the message that is most often forgotten. Upon entry to the city we immediately became aware this was the city of death. This was the city we would most likely to be killed in.

There were more bobby-traps around this city and possibly in it then any I could remember, I do not know why it was so well fortified as it was seemingly insignificant as far as strong holds would go. We knew of nothing special about it or in it, there was nothing in any intelligence reports about it or any suspected enemy stronghold. But with all the security it must have something going on inside it and it was now our self-appointed mission to find out just what the hell it was. Whether or not anyone would live through this visit to tell about it was questionable. In the first few hours we disconnected and neutralized what seemed to be hundreds booby traps and land mines, maybe that was a stretch, but it seemed like the fact. There was booby -traps that looked like swinging gates covered with punji sticks and poisoned, attached by a trip wire that was barely visible. These were set at waist high and would completely destroy the entire upper torso. Then there were pressure release anti-personnel mines buried just waiting for someone to step on. Locating these and disarming them was a long arduous and tedious task. There was a pit that was covered and looked like it was part of the natural landscape and had never been disturbed; you had to be really good to see it was a covered pit; the tip off was it was too pristine for a well-traveled area. In the pit were numerous punji sticks sharpened and poisoned just waiting for someone to fall in. Many an American service man had gone down because of this one. Damn these bastards were good at setting up booby-traps, and they had taken many lives with little material, mostly materials we had given them, or we had haphazardly discarded or they had stolen from us. As stated several times as much as I deplored these bastards, I respected them and their ability to do so much with so little, there was no waste material to them, only used items that could have another use. Everything we discarded they could reuse. Finally after what seemed like days we were able to disarm and in many cases disassemble many or most of the mines and bobby traps so it would be safe for the infantry to come marching in. This was a village known to have been frequented by the Viet Cong. A couple more days and we would turn it over to the regular infantry and we were out of here. Our mission complete, we called in the infantry and sure enough this was a Viet Cong stronghold where there were numerous guns and grenades with enough ammunition to sustain a small army for several days. The odd thing was the enemy was nowhere around, no signs of them having been there by the actions of the people. Generally if the Viet Cong had been through a village and then we showed up the people were nervous and acted really skittish. With this much fire- power they had to be somewhere just lying in wait for us to leave. You could literally feel eyes on you peering into your very heart and just waiting, just wanting for the right opportunity, after all they were going nowhere, this was their home, we were the outsiders. Engineers were called in and they destroyed the entire cache of weapons and ammunition so they would be of no use to them. The explosives or ammunition they had was so powerful when ignited it rocked the ground for many hours. There was no way they could not have known, even if the trees had blind eyes and all the people were deaf. This was a definite set-up and all the villagers were part of it, down to the last young child.

Fortunately it was time for us to leave, and the Infantry Unit to take over, had it been up to us they would have all been destroyed for having led us into this ambush without remorse.

A Pathetic Waste

In any war a lot of money and materials are used, wasted, gave away, and some flat out stolen, but in some places we find there is a complete and inexcusable waste of good materials. As I watched in my spirit world, someplace in-between reality and dream world I watched as perfectly good M-14 rifles were placed in a big ditch and an engineer went across them with a cutting torch, cutting them in three sections and burying them. The rifles were escorted to this sight and then under guard until the cutting process was started. Often Viet Cong would sneak in and steal these perfectly good guns for use against us. Even though the movement of these weapons was kept hush -hush, somehow the destination and location was always learned and there were generally a few firefights to test the strength of the unit guarding or escorting. If it was obvious they were a small contingency thinking no one knew what they were carrying then they would rain down on them like the monsoon, destroy them and take the equipment whatever it may be, helping us to help them to extend the war efforts.

The tremendous amount of the rifles and the shape they were in appalled me, since many our own troops were fighting with Army rejects, they were literally destroying better guns then we had in the field. God forbid you try to trade; some clerk in an office somewhere in the rear with the beer freak out since he had a roster of each rifle and he would not dare compromise his roster. Hell most of us had traded our weapons dozens of times in the bush; no one knew what their original rifle number was. Hell many of the bush soldiers were carrying AK-47's themselves as they could fire the enemies rounds and our ammunition as well.

If I was appalled at the amount and quality of rifles destroyed I was beside myself when they started to drive perfectly good jeeps in the hole to bury. I would have loved to have had one of them at home in Kentucky to go driving through the woods hunting and getting to some of the better fishing spots. The sick fact is they were in better shape then most of the Marine units had, but still in the hole they went for destruction and burial. This seemed radically wasteful and just tore at every fiber of my being. How wasteful our government is and then we talk about raising taxes to make up the government shortages after wasting all this fine equipment. If mainstream society ever seen all this waste they would freak out! They really would have a justified reason to demonstrate, instead of some bullshit excuse some want to be veterans made up. I asked several times, but as with all government bureaucracy, nobody seemed to know exactly who ordered this destruction, just that they had written orders to destroy these items and even serial numbers of items to be destroyed. I could not help but wonder if we were actually here to help the South Vietnamese then why did we not give all this good equipment to them instead of destroying it. There must have been some good reason and I was just too far down the food chain to get the answers, or even considered as significant enough to have the right to ask questions.

My only concern was to get my butt out of this place alive and in one piece with all my parts. I could just feel us being watched every second of everyday. There was just way too much movement not to have someone seeing and watching us. The heavy equipment operators worked around the clock to completely bury the jeeps, then another vast ditch was dug and 21/2 trucks were brought in, and this is when all hell broke loose. It was now not just suspect, but it was real and we found out in a hurry, the enemy was not only watching, but also doing a kind of shopping trip, they were waiting for what they wanted and then they attacked. They hit us so hard and so fast, we were completely surprised and several of the trucks were taken, we blew out as many as we could while they were driving away, but a few good trucks did get out. No down payment, no contract, and no finance charges, theirs clear and free and to the cost of the average Joe taxpayer. Several good men died that day for the price of a discarded vehicle. I could not help but wonder what a vehicle like this would bring in the black market, it was without a doubt more then a life was worth. Of course there was not much value to a life or several lives here and now in this land of death and destruction.

Life is temporal and best we can hope for is to die without suffering too much. Just as in the days of Nimrod at the tower of Babel, when a building stone was more prized then a human life, an implement of war was much prized over a human being. War changes who we are and what we value most, that is just plain and simple fact, be it good or bad, just what it is, Fact! Just as construction workers and repairmen value their tools and become very skilled at using them so to does a combat soldier, he becomes very proficient at using his tool, a rifle, and his life depends on his skill. After a while it does not matter if you are building up something, tearing it down or eradicating the enemy soldier, it becomes a job and the better you are at it the better your chances of coming out of this alive are. As it has been beat in our heads, it is not for you as a professional to give your life for your country, but to have the enemy give his life for his country. Up to this point we had become very proficient at it and each night you survived was a testament to your proficiency and of course your luck as well. No matter how proficient you are there is still the chance of you just being in the wrong place at the wrong time and your luck running out.

In war the warrior is not the one to blame for the blatant waste and disregard for loss of life associated with the procurement of equipment and supplies. When governments openly display waste at such mammoth levels, then the people in need feel it only right to take from them what they waste and would not otherwise be able to find. Sadly enough through the procurement of this equipment and supplies there is collateral damage, people are killed and die just to get to the stuff that is needed to survive. When this occurs a letter is sent to the loved ones talking about how this or that person died for his country, when reality is they died to protect the outward waste our government demonstrated in front of a people that has nothing. These are the folks that pick C-ration boxes out of the dump to fill with dirt and use to build their hooch's. How honorable is this. And the beat goes on! Again this is waste the news media never reports, waste of materials we as warriors could have used, if for no other reason then barter. Equip your allies and teach them to fight, after all that was the original plan.

Again I was somehow in another place at yet another time

and situation still whirling from the most recent experience and wondering how I was somewhat responsible. It was a tremendous waste to issue substandard M-16's when we had good solid weapons, the M-14 and Steven shotguns. This was undoubtedly a means of supporting pork barrel companies by giving them contracts for these substandard weapons. I do agree we need to support our businesses in the United States to keep the money flowing, but this was an atrocious waste of criminal proportion and not one word from the press. There was no mention how these new weapons were causing the death of thousands of our own service members because of misfires and jamming. Prototypes and new weaponry should not be tested in combat as lives are at stake; they need to be tested by personnel in the rear away from the enemy and the fear of loss of life if the new equipment fails.

A Place Called Emptiness

As I looked around me I realized I had entered a place of total emptiness, a place void of all life. There was no grass minus the burnt, dry, brown spots long dead waiting a good storm to blow it away. There were no trees, no animals, no people, with exception of us, and my thoughts made me wonder if even we were real or just thoughts traveling on a road to nowhere accomplishing nothing. We too were empty, free of feeling, free of emotion, free of life in general, just walking dead men that have not realized we should just lie down and accept we are dead. There was not even life under the rocks! The hills were dead from the actions and sound of war, completely void of all life; there were no sounds of birds or any other living things. This after all is the direct result of war, total and complete ruination. Destruction of everything and everyone completely void, utter and total destruction, of even plant and animal life stretched over miles of real estate.

If this was the plan, then success was in hand, it was desolate! We still walked cautiously through this desolation just waiting for the sound that would end this existence or mission. Sadly enough we sometimes welcomed it yet it would not come and relieve us of the pain, we were the lucky ones we would survive to live this experience over and over again in our hearts and minds. The lyrics of a favorite song of the Vietnam veteran begins to pound in my head as we cross this dead mans land void of all life, WAR! Uh, yeah, What is it good for, Absolutely nothing, War it ain't nothing but a heartbreaker, friend to only the undertaker, It's an enemy to all mankind, the point of war blows my mind, War has caused unrest to the younger generation, Induction then destruction, Who wants to die?

This epitomizes war at its highest level or lowest, contingent upon what level you are viewing it from. People will generally work things out, not always, but generally, Governments will wage war and then send the innocent people to fight the wars for them, and then have the audacity to say, look how well we done! This is by no means a new concept, if history is true and sometimes that is questionable because of bias of the scribes just like with the news media of today. Then slaves would be taken and forced to fight for their Masters to earn their freedom. We would like to color it different from modern day warriors, but when you think about it, how different is it? We take the lower caste and the working poor and even the middle class whatever that may mean, and we send them off to war to fight to save our country or for the cause of freedom in some other country because we feel it is our duty to ensure global freedom. This sadly enough is a generalization that if we eliminate the lower caste in war, they have honor and our government will not have to support them through welfare or other domestic government programs and as a secondary advantage, we cut back on the gangs as it is the poor and downtrodden that form gangs in order to protect themselves and to acquire their needs and then as they grow in strength and numbers most of their wants. They even justify it as taking away from the rich fat cats and giving to the people in need, their brothers and fellow gang members. If the government stayed out of it, they would ultimately kill themselves off through turf wars.

Poor leadership leads to poor decisions and the uneducated and needy make poor leaders because of their need to feel self-worth, which too often distracts from the mission at hand and generates power struggles among themselves. Truth be told there can never be total freedom without anarchy, and we cannot have too much freedom, or there will not be the workers to provide for the wealthy. There would be no one to collect the trash, clean their yards and homes, pick the fruits and vegetables, and clean their cars and even build their houses.

All this as it is, but there is one fact that remains vivid at this very point in time at this very moment, we are walking on land that once flourished with vegetation and now it was totally desolate and completely void of all vegetation and life as we know it, was this what the cost of freedom would be? Complete and total emptiness! I too was starting to feel the very same way, totally empty and void of emotion and feelings.

The mind is a wonderful thing, just as I was starting to feel depressed and in some funny way violated, we broke for the night and I dozed off. I began to dream of this place called home that seemed so far away and almost non-existent. I dreamed of Mary and the life we would have when this was all over and I returned home as in the old song," When Johnny Comes marching home again! I dreamed of the eight to five job, the three- bedroom house and the white picket fence, the station wagon or mini-van in the driveway and the three children, two boys and a girl. Shopping on

Saturday, maybe a movie, a visit to the local burger joint as a special treat for the family, burgers and fries and even splurge and have a milk shake to go with it. The evening hours would be at home with the family helping with the homework, talking to each other as a family, maybe a cookout or just a nice meal and television before bedtime. Then up early for Church and maybe a movie, or the beach. But it was not the same, and it would never be the same, why even try to bullshit myself, there was little respect for what we were doing and when we come marching home we would be coming home to unemployment and financially hard times. People suspected we were all drug addicts and Mary had run off with Jody. For the here and now it was important that I believed life went forward in a positive manner and look through rose- colored glasses. Although we were the same age as many of the folks in college and starting new jobs, we were somehow much older. We had seen so much we would never be able to explain to anyone and especially to those we loved, they mostly thought we were all crazy killers. Granted we had seen and done our share of killing, but that did not make us killers, we did this for our country and the cause at least that is what they taught us and continued to pound in our heads. But what cause? Somehow it seems to escape my memory as the killing continues. Most of us would end up with a couple of divorces, heavy drinkers, drugs, jail and for some prison, few friends and for many dropping out of mainstream society and living in the boonies away from cities and out in the bush where we knew how to survive. When I awoke, I was still in the land of emptiness, the land God forgot, at least the God I was taught about. Where I ask was this God when I needed him or it, when I asked for things where was he she or it? I was taught ask and you will receive but there was even a curve to that analogy, it must be his will, how the hell was I to know his will, and why did it appear as if it must be immensely different from what my wants and needs were. We are taught that he will fulfill our needs, not so much our wants but our needs. So who determines what are needs and which are wants. My home is a need so I can provide for my family and their physical needs, but then when you are poor you have to fight to keep some big business from stealing your home because you can not get financing because of some scam or red tape. As much as we the lower caste are beaten up and oppressed, we are the ones who go marching off to war, what if we had a war and all the poor went to Canada or refused to fight to support the rich fat cats? But I for one still want to believe we in America can still work hard and get ahead. We can become someone if we work hard and apply our talents. Does anyone really want to hear what we have to say?

The Tunnel Rat

ere I was again swooped off to some other area and another operation or mission completely blinded of what the next experience was to be, just knowing it would be something else I did not want to be reminded of. A life and a world I had struggled to suppress and even forget was again about to be thrown back into my face another time. With the so called head shed, the heavy duty zero's, Commanders of the units and theater, an Operation and mission were largely different, Operations went down in the history books and were designated from higher powers, but missions were daily occurrences, standard operating procedures. To us, the grunts, they were all the same and death loomed over each and every one of us with each and every one of these missions or operations.

Everyone was loaded up, packs swollen with food and equipment for the mission, sitting on the helicopter pad awaiting the choppers to pick us up and drop us at our designated drop zone somewhere in the middle of nowhere land, maybe Laos, Cambodia, or Vietnam, hell we did not know the difference, all we knew was our number could come up at any time or place at any minute, either enemy or friendly. It really did not matter as dead was still dead. We were all briefed on the mission, but it really did not mean

186

anything to us, just SOS, same old shit as usual. Our only concern was since we were so well briefed, was all the other troops in the area briefed on where we were? It was like going deer hunting; someone sees movement and opens fire never knowing whom they are shooting at. The intelligence reports we were given was never correct and we often wondered if just maybe they got them from Ouigi board or something as obscure, military intelligence truly is an oxymoron. Truth is no one anywhere really knew shit and the ones that professed they did made it up as they went. We in the bush gave the correct and honest reports, but by the time the information filtered up the chain of command it was completely different, everyone wanted to add to it what they suspected and assumed. Assume was just as it was spelled, ass u me, their assumptions made Asses out of you and me and often was the cause of many a death because someone in the chain of command wanted to feel important and add to or take away what was reported. I remember sitting in a briefing one day and hearing the intelligence reports and they sounded completely foreign to me, then I found out these were the reports my team submitted, and there was no similarity to what we reported. I actually thought there had been some drastic changes in the last couple days we never heard of as we were just peons anyhow.

Finally, an hour or so later then we were told, we hear the thump, thump, thump of the helicopter blades as it slowly descended to the pad for us to load on to. This would be the last time this helicopter would actually touch the ground on this particular mission, when it dropped us off it would be moving and we would jump off in sequence as it lifted and was out of the area in seconds of it's arrival. Almost immediately after the drop off we had to call for a medical evacuation since one of the Corporals broke his ankle as he jumped out of the helicopter. After we set up a hasty defensive position we called in the medical evacuation and awaited their arrival. Meanwhile a couple small recon missions were being run to see what we could actually expect to run into. We needed real life reports and not the crap we received at the intelligence briefings. Finally the medical evacuation helicopter arrives and the young Corporal is taken away to survive another day out of the field and possibly because of this, another day in the world of the living. As for us the mission must go on. We started to move out headed towards these grid coordinates that were passed down from higher command, and we arrived just before sundown. We set up the perimeter guards and established firing lanes. Wire was run around the perimeter both German and barbed wire. Then the communications folks strung wire for the radios. We were in business and ready to operate. We would run short-range recon missions off this Operation Position; we would be looking for tunnels. Although I was thin, I was very thankful to be six foot tall, this meant I was too tall for the tunnels, and being tunnel rat was a deadly job, you could be blown up by booby traps, or run right into the enemy on your way down. No guarantees you were coming out alive. We would tie a rope around the waist of the tunnel rat and if he pulled the rope we knew we had to get him out as rapidly as possible. Suffice it to say the odds were against him surviving even one tunnel much less a complete tour. Of course there were those that would beat the odds, but very few of them. They had to wonder if they would run into enemy soldiers, snakes and other wild animals, booby traps and a myriad of other things that would lead to immediate death, and they were down there alone with no way for anyone to get to them in a hurry. These were true heroes and very brave men. Here we are somewhere in the jungle somewhere in Vietnam or was it Laos or Cambodia, I have no idea, neither did most of non-rates and truth be known we really did not care, it was all the same to us, the grim reaper hiding behind every stone, bush and cave. All we knew we were at grid coordinates such and such as though that really meant anything to us with exception of the fact we knew where to have the medical evacuation chopper land if it came to that. We would only be out a couple days if all went as planned. As luck or misfortune would have it, we found a bunker heavily armed with booby traps, and it led to a tunnel. After it was defused the tunnel rat would go in, it seemed he had been in for way too long when he started pulling on the rope and we began to pull him out as fast as we could, we pulled faster and faster with the sudden fear he was not alive as the rope went taunt and it seemed we were dragging him. This was one of five enemy soldiers that would be dragged out of the tunnel with their throats cut, then finally the tunnel rat was pulled out, he had smiles from head to toe. Barely five feet and 110 probably soaking wet and he had just personally killed in hand-to-hand combat five of the enemy soldiers. After he came out we dropped hand grenades into the tunnel and called in artillery directly on top of it. It was used, as a storage cache for weapons and these weapons would serve no purpose for them as they were destroyed and we made sure of it. Another of our unsung heroes saves some of our troops from being destroyed with these weapons at least. Life in the field goes on to find another cache or even better, one of the underground cities. Some of these tunnel dwellers lived for decades under ground, digging and building, never seeing the light of day. It was amazing what these people could do with so little.

LZ English Hill 173

Again I was taken to another area and yet another operation, it was beginning to seem there was no end to the destruction and death. Here we were on another desolate hill in the middle of nowhere, another place where I could see no reasonable need for us to be. Some how in their infinite wisdom the powers above me seen it as a significant point of interest. There were several young men and they were set up like so many other Lz's, landing zones, all throughout the country. Around the perimeter at varying intervals were pits with sandbagged bunkers and a small hole with an M-60 machine gun pointed out ward with fire lanes established and set. A bunker was located in the middle for the communications people and the command bunker next to it. Because there was not a lot of real estate, plus it was convenient for the commander to be next to his communications section in case of incoming calls or the necessity to make immediate calls for artillery, naval gunfire or air power, not to mention medical evacuations.

It was a miserably hot and humid day like so many others as the commander assigned tasks to the troops. There were those that would be stringing wire, as we called it, putting up German concertina with barbed wire strung through it and tied down to the ground with stakes. There were those

191

designated to emplace grenades with the pins straightened out, and this was a bit touchy, as one pull on the wire after the pin was straightened then the whole mess would go up in one big blast of flying metal fragments, needless to say, you never attached the grenades with the straightened pins until the work was complete and no one was pulling on the wire. There was another crew outside the perimeter burning off any vegetation that might reduce visibility, and they would also be responsible for digging holes just outside the burned off area for listening posts a night, the forward observation positions, the place where so many soldiers had their throats cut if they should doze off or was not listening really close for any type of movement.

After a couple hours, everything starts to sound alike it just becomes a hum. You just never really knew when or if you would be taken out. Some were to ration out water and food for the day, not the most popular people in the world as we always wanted more then we got but everyone understood we all had a job to do and if we were not rationed we would inevitably come up short.

It seemed the whole tour of duty in Vietnam we were just a little bit hungry, not starving, but at that point where you could use just a bit more to eat with the exception of a few special occasions. There were a couple operations or missions where we were extended and our food supply was dropped in the enemies laps and we had to go without and eat whatever we could find, we felt like we were going to starve to death. We were even taking food off the dead enemy to eat.

Then there was the corpsman or medic that would go around and ensure we were all in the best shape we could be in given the current situation. He would issue out salt pills and ensure we were drinking adequate amounts of water. That really was not much of a problem as long as we had the water since it was ungodly hot and we sweat like horses. There were occasions where there was no water and we had to find it and I can remember drinking the green brackish water of creeks and other waterways in Vietnam. I can also remember the diarrhea that came afterward, but it was far better then dying of thirst. You can go a lot longer and farther without food then you can water. Of course there was the fortunate couple assigned to burning the shitter, oh! What a glorious job that was, you smelled like kerosene and shit for a week afterwards, then it was time to do it all over again. The way it was done is one man would pour kerosene in the fifty -five gallon drum that had been cut in half and a wooden seat attached, the seat would be taken off and set aside, then another would stir it in real good and then it would be lit, after that it would be stirred a few more times to ensure it was completely burned out for sanitation purposes. It would burn all day long and the smell would permeate the area, this made for real tasty meals. There was the morning briefing by the Commander he would direct lines of fire and all that good West Point stuff, that would last about a week and then it would die out as it always did, mostly because it was the same thing everyday and you can only say the same thing so many ways until you run out of ways to say it.

In the communications shack were two fairly new guys all of eighteen, with all the communications equipment, and this was generally one of the first targets the enemy would try to take out, no communication and you are in deep poop! Their mission was maintain all communications equipment and to climb the pole and put up wire to enhance communications. God only knows we must have put up a million yards of landline or what was called slash wire throughout Vietnam, Cambodia and Laos, sadly enough we would often find it used as trip wires as well.

On this particular day one of the young lads was to climb the pole and hook up the slash wire, to where or why I have no idea, but the other young man was to take the truck a 2 ½ ton commonly called a 6 by or deuce and a half, go to the supply area in the rear, about twenty miles away and pick up some supplies. This would be a walk in the park, a piece of cake, pretty much a restful day while everyone else was busting humps (working) in the hot sun digging holes, filling sand bags and fortify positions around the perimeter. Everything seemed to be going as planned. One of the young men hated to climb poles and was not very good at it so he asked if he could make the run and the other agreed, he would stay behind and climb poles while his buddy went on a cake walk to the village. This was a decision that would haunt the one who agreed to stay behind and climb poles for the rest of his life.

The day was progressing as well as could be expected considering the current situation, and it must have been about ten in the morning judging from the position of the sun and the sundial that had been built for shits and grins. One of the college graduates Lieutenants ideas and pet projects. Of course this was the Lieutenant that believed he had lived long ago and was a roman centurion. This convoy of trucks came into the compound and said there had been a truck that had hit a landmine and it was reported it was the communications specialist that had left our compound. They needed someone to go to graves registration to identify the body. Graves Registration was anything but what the title implied it was a morgue where they would take the dead bodies, embalm them and try to identify them before they would send the bodies to the mainland where they would be escorted to their location in their hometown. The place was cold, for obvious reasons I learned, and reminded me of Frankenstein's workshop with body parts lying around everywhere arms legs, etc... The Graves Registration personnel would do their best to match up the body part to the right person. It would be the other communications man they would send to identify the body since he knew the person best, he would be leaving with the convoy on there return, which would be sometime after noon. Off they went, about ten miles into the trip, right in front of them was about four jeeps with body parts spread all over the area, they had been ambushed or hit one hell'uva a mine. Everyone had to dismount and collect body parts, and dog tags, the pieces of metal that were worn around the neck or in the boots taped together. They would then put whatever body parts they could find or scrap together put them into body bags and carried with them to graves registration. Finally arriving at graves registration, reports had to be filled out and the body parts turned over to graves registration people. There was information about who you were where the bodies were found, and as best possible a detailed report of what happened. This was at best speculation as we had just accidentally come upon the carnage. Then the even tougher part for the young communications specialist, he was led into this cold room and shown the body of his buddy, he had somehow hoped it would not be him, but sadly enough it was him, recognizable enough to make a positive identification.

That night they would be put up in base quarters since it was getting dark and no one traveled at night, other then the Viet Cong. There were only three or four men there and the other men were going on Rest and Recuperation to Thailand for a week out of country. One was a sergeant, and this was his second tour. Somewhere around midnight or one in the morning, at it's darkest point, a sapper ran into the quarters and threw a satchel charge into the hutch, the young sergeant jumped on top of it having his body blown to pieces saving our lives. His R&R was cut short, he would never see Thailand or home again, most say he was a hero, and I too feel he was but what reward does a hero get? Medals for his family to place beside his picture, what comforts will that bring his mother? He was awarded the Medal of Honor the highest medal our nation has to offer for saving our worthless lives, I never really knew this man, but I would never forget him, he gave his life to save mine. Sadly enough his family would get the big insurance policy of ten thousand dollars, a medal, a letter from the Commanding Officer and a folded flag for the service this man gave his country. There was an old saying that there are those that pass through our lives for a season or a reason, I guess this was his reason, but how sad it was for him to give his life in a country we had not even heard of a few years ago for a cause that was unclear, but we were told and convinced initially it was to stop the counterinsurgency of communist forces in southeast Asia. IT sounded good in the beginning, then as time passed and you seen death almost daily you begin to ask yourself what the hell it even meant. Hell most of us never heard of or know what counterinsurgency means so many that paid the price were almost if not totally literate, but they had heart. They loved there country and had so little when so many with so much complained the most about there way of life in this country we were fighting to preserve, a way of life. The war continues on and we pack up for yet another adventure here in the far eastern games of survival!

Back to Hill 146

ere we were again on Hill 146, I had seen and heard of so many of our young men being killed and wounded on this God forsaken hill. It did not look like anything special, just another hill with a parapet dug completely around it cut off with barbed wire and German concertina and void of all vegetation. For us who knew the story of the blood shed and actually a couple of us had shed some blood on this godforsaken hill, it had a very special meaning. Most of the time we just set up on the hill ran short- range recon patrols off the hill gathering whatever information we could. Generally speaking we found little to nothing worthwhile, but the young Officers that went on the missions with us always found something to report, mostly to make themselves look good. Some really exaggerated to the degree we thought they were writing fiction books but it was enough to where we were extended waiting arrival of one of the Infantry units. Or worse yet, they would have the jets drop bombs in areas we never seen anything just to say they had come into contact and had to call for backup the shit got so deep, the shit was definitely deep, but we would just go along with the program as our duty was to protect our young officers. Granted exaggeration is a way of life with most men, but it is different when others lives are placed in jeopardy so someone can get an expedited promotion. This was not always the case, as I said early on I have known some awesome Officers, and many truly were leaders and heroes, but most of them were Mustanger's, (prior enlisted men). One really can not blame these young Officers, they are brainwashed from day one to believe they are the true leaders, truth be known, leaders are not born, they are made through adversity, challenges, and sadly enough mistakes.

The Non Commissioned Officer's will teach them the way if they are smart enough to listen. In the bush it is not rank that determines who is in charge, but mostly the experience. It is often the buck sergeant who is on his third tour in Vietnam that knows the real scoop and will get you through your mission and back alive. The month or so passes and you are again in the rear with the beer and playing guard duty, mess duty and all that garrison bullshit you stayed in the bush to stay away from. They say there is no such thing as bush Marines and garrison Marines, but I must disagree as I knew some fine combat bush Marines but they just could not deal with Garrison spit and polish duty. Give them a rifle and put them in the bush and there will be none better.

This time on this particular hill all hell was going to break loose and we would loose some fine young men who had aged too much before their time. The first sign something was up happened just before sunset, I heard a crack, crack, crack and I looked over and a sniper had taken out our senior Corpsman, then the dog handler, which meant we had to take down the dog, although a sad situation, if the dog handler is killed, the dog has to be killed unless he can be retrained to another master, and in the bush you have no time. Our lieutenant was next, and they just continued to pick off our men and we could not see the muzzle flash, and the valley distorted the sound so we could not even tell where it was coming from except for the trajectory if we could see the impact as it occurred. Otherwise we would not be able to tell since the body would jerk and more often flop so it was now out of the direction it was hit from. The only real hope of getting this sniper was when the darkness set in we would be able to see the muzzle flash, but how many would he take out before dark, we must stay down, but things had to be done before the night games commenced. Then just as rapidly as the sniper started, it stopped, and we would not be able to make this bastard pay for the ones he killed, he or she would go unpunished, at least in this world for this time. We all knew this was merely a sign that all hell was about to break loose that night and no one would have to exaggerate, but then we had no zeros (common slang reference to military Officers by enlisted men) with us, good old sarge was in charge again, but then he always was anyhow, even the" LT"(lieutenant) knew it and was okay with it as sarge had been here for three years straight and most of that time in the bush where he excelled and felt most comfortable.

Old Sarge was a really good man, he really was not that old, only in his twenties, but older then us. He could be a righteous asshole sometimes. That was because he took things so seriously, every crack or sound meant something and if you stayed with him and learned, he would teach you things you could never imagine, ways of surviving and allowing the enemy to die for his country instead of you dying for yours. Sarge was from somewhere in Kentucky I had never even heard of and I was born in Louisville Kentucky. Rumor was he ran off and joined the Marine

Corps after getting drunk one night and beating a man to death in a bar fight which in those days was very probable as many a Marine was on the wrong side of the law prior to entering, this was the sixties. If you worked with him in the bush it would not be hard for you to believe. He was the quietest thing in the bush, I say thing because not even an animal could be as quiet as him, it was almost like the old Tarzan movies, and he was raised by the apes and learned his stealth and jungle savvy from them. He told us and I totally believed it that mother Nature would speak to him, I was convinced of it. He could look at a broken branch and tell just how long it had been since it was broken and how heavy the item or being was that had broken it from the way it was broken. He could stand back and look at a shallow water way and see the path most recently taken by the displacement of the rocks and mud displaced in the bed of the waterway. He even fished this same way, some type of relationship or bond with nature, he would wade into the water in a certain spot where he knew there would be fish, say some kind of chant, watch very quietly and stand like a frozen statue then reach in the water and grab a fish right out of the water so fast the fish would not even realize he had it in his hands. Some questioned whether he was a witch or a reincarnated Indian (now Native American to be politically correct) scout or hunter from a past life here in the present. Many had seen him sneak up on the enemy and snap their necks before they realized he was even there. He was wicked with a knife and had made him a bow and arrows, which he was deadly with and could kill a person with them never knowing what hit them or where it came from. His innate ability to create comfort items out of gifts Mother Nature provided made field duty very comfortable. He was also a lot like a MacGyver, he could make just about anything from nothing, and he made some of the most complex and strange booby traps I had ever seen and definitely could not imagine. He also had some evil methods for getting the enemy to talk and never leave a mark. On the same token, he could kill a person and you would never know how they died. He was a natural pharmacist or herbalist if you will, he could mix nutritious spices for seasoning, roots and plants that would give you energy better then a sports nutritionist. He had cures for diarrhea, constipation, stomachache and almost anything else that ailed you. Sarge was truly a warrior and one you definitely wanted on your side and not against you. The enemy called him the Ghost Killer as they never seen him but they seen his work.

Old Sarge told us all hell was going to break loose somewhere between two and four in the morning. How he knew we had no idea but we knew if he said it that is what was going to happen. He then placed us on 50% watch until about one thirty, then he woke everyone and had us on100% alert. This meant every man would be awake, weapon locked and loaded prepared for a sudden rush of the enemy. He was, as always, right, around two in the morning they started to drop mortars in on us, and then around three they started to come up over the perimeter wire, one man or woman would run forward lay down on the wire, almost certain death, they the rest would run over top of them. They were stoned and their limbs had been bound so they could not feel the pain. Many of the soldiers had satchel charges attached to them, their mission was to destroy and take as many with them as they could. This night they would be severely disappointed as Old Sarge had out smarted them and we tore them apart with only minor wounds the Corpsman would fix and send these wounded back to his place on the line. We had many men wounded in the bush but most never got a Purple Heart because no entry was ever made in their records and some did not want any because three Purple Hearts and they pulled you out of the field, we had no glory hounds, they will eventually get you killed and generally sooner then later, these were warriors, they needed the field and the war. I could not help but wonder what was going to happen when the war was over and they had no war to fight. Of course, I knew America needed another war somewhere, and that meant there would always be war, after all we were a peaceful people but we needed war to prove it, we needed war to prove our God was greater then someone else's God and we needed war to prove our way of life was superior to every one else's. That is just the way it is our economy needs war, war helps thin out the people just as natures fires clear the forest and the floods regurgitated the garbage from the rivers lakes and streams to cleanse itself and thin out the amount of garbage mankind and other nature had put in it.

"Private Numb Nuts"

Private Numb nuts was undoubtedly the most screwed up dysfunctional man I had ever met, if there were 999 ways to do something right and only one to do it wrong, he would somehow manage to screw it up. He was one of the Category 4 Marines that had a GT of dirt, which meant he was basically untrainable. The only thing we could hope for was to give him a rifle and show him which direction he should aim it in and pull the trigger. It seemed like no matter what you gave him to do he would somehow mess up and then could not understand why everyone was down on him. The worse part is he would try to make up for his screw up and it would only make matters worse then they already were. He was a nice guy, kind of timid, very shy and he really did mean to do well. I do not know how he managed to get through boot camp, especially Marine Corps boot camp, but then this was the sixties and the Marines needed warm bodies to serve in Vietnam. Here he was our personal screw-up, a product of the need for warm bodies to use as cannon fodder.

Private Numb nuts spent less time in the bush then most, and more time on mess and guard then anyone else. Of course as the luck of the draw would have it, we seemed to end up with him most. He did not intentionally screw-up, it was just this curse or something that seemed to follow him around. Just like the rest of us, Private Numbnuts had a mission and we would all learn what that mission was.

One night we were on a fairly large operation and our objective was to take this hill so we could be on the high ground. There was also a large weapons supply route reported in this area. We were moving at a healthy pace when all hell broke loose, we could not seem to get up the hill as a machine gun nest had us pinned down, and we were pinned down good. All we could do is try to out wait the gun and their ammunition or try to out fight the enemy and take out a lot more of them then they took of us. This was getting to be a bad choice as the enemy was moving in mass and towards us, and there had to be three times as many of them as us, seemingly standard odds for Marines. From the perspective of the average troop it appeared as if two would appear every time you killed one of them and it did seem as though this math would continue on for eternity. I did not know there was this many well trained soldiers in all South Vietnam, they just kept coming. I began to appreciate the stories I would hear from the Korean War veterans where they would continue to kill the enemy and they would continue to march forward over the dead masses and towards you, and each time one fell three appeared. All we could do is try to get the enemy to move off to our right flank so we could slip up the left and neutralize the machine gun position, but they were not moving in that direction as rapidly as we needed them to. Matter of fact is they were not moving at all from all outward appearances.

Out of nowhere Private Numb nuts jumped up and started running towards the bunker, as he arrives at the top of the bunker after taking out several enemy soldiers along the way, he is wounded twice, but keeps focused on taking out the machine gun nest. He thrusts himself forward throwing a grenade inside the bunker and then jumps up on top of the bunker and takes out the position along with the machine gun single handedly. It was an incredible act of bravery and one that was definitely not expected of Private Numbnuts. We were now free to move forward. After arriving at the bunker, we were all sitting taking a breather before we moved on when a grenade rolled out of the bunker and the spoon flew off, we were all standing there and soon to be Swiss cheese, however Private Numbnuts already shot up and dying, Private Numbnuts dove on it saving the lives of dozens of Marines. Private Numbnuts was immediately blown to pieces.

Private Numbnuts was awarded the Medal of Honor for his gallant bravery above and beyond the call of duty giving his life for his fellow Marines and saving the lives of so many of his comrade in arms, and a Purple Heart. He earned our respect and that of all Marines present and future. He was the least expected to have ever thought of doing such a thing, but he had saved the lives of his fellow Marines and become a hero among heroes! Heroes come in assorted packages and I was convinced of this with Private Numbnuts, I think he had taught each and everyone of us a lesson this day. No one would ever talk stink about him again, and he would go down in history, but more then that he would be our hero, having saved our lives from certain death. He would be remembered as a hero to our families for all time.

Prior to entering the Marines Private Numbnuts was destined to end up on welfare or in prison, he was a natural born loser and looked down on by all the towns people, made fun of when he was in school and yet inside he was always a hero just waiting for the right time and place to present itself and in all probability he did not even know it, it was just always there and choices he made led him to where he was and destiny took over. How many Private Numbnuts are out there in Prisons, and on the streets homeless because the opportunity or situation never availed itself because of decisions made or not made? I suspect numerous, matter of fact I believe heroes are merely heroes because of where they are and when they are there and mostly because of reaction to a given action and not because they intended to become heroes but through necessity and a stimulus response. We look down on people because they are different, when in fact the difference is what makes them unique and special. It is like that very special vase, it is most special because of its character, and that is because it is different.

What is sad is now Private Numbnuts will be the local town hero and all will remember his name, but before he went off and gave his life he was not even known to the vast amount of people in the town and many of those that did know him only knew him as the town bum or idiot. The bullies would pick on him and he rarely had enough to eat, children would throw rocks at him and the system turned a blind eye. . Now he was special, in death he gained life, he became someone, families talked about the brave young man from their hometown that went off to war and gave his life. If he would have stayed home and lived life he would have been a dead man merely passing from one day to the next. The joke of the city, the town idiot, every town has one. The other sad reality is it is not Private Numbnuts that the community honors, but the notoriety brought to them by him. His name will be etched on the veteran's wall in the town center and eventually with time and weather the memory will fade and he will, as with all veterans be a passing memory to only those who are family or seek notoriety from him having been in the family line. We are Americans, but are we fading as fast as the memories and names of those who fought and died to keep this country free? Welcome Home!

Christmas In The Bush

Christmas in the bush was much like any other day, with but a few exceptions. We made the most out of it and in our simple way with our limited means did celebrate the day the best we could. We found a tree, definitely not an evergreen, but any tree would work, after all it is not the tree that has the has the significance, the tree is merely a symbol of a time we remember that was good for us. The tree we found had stickers all over it so we acquainted it to the crown of thorns Jesus was forced to wear and the pain and suffering we could to a degree associate with. We decorated he tree with grenades, empty C-Ration cans, and the brass from the M-60 machine gun. It may not have looked like much but to us on top of a desolate hill in the middle of nowhere land away from our families and loved ones with meager means and a probability we would not see the light of day it was pretty awesome and for a brief moment lightened our hearts and brought us joy.

Joy is one of those fleeting things we could only get in small servings here in good old Vietnam. There was the allotment of two beers per person helo lifted to our OP and even a special meal, so we did the best we could to make it a memorable day, we gave what we had to each other, maybe a c-ration pack of cigarettes, I think there were four in it,

209

usually chesterfield, lucky strike or camel non-filters. It was a sad time, mostly a day when we all left each other alone so we could reminisce about our loved ones back home and what we would probably be doing if we were there with them. Christmas and family are in our minds and would always be there so for that day we allowed ourselves the luxury of just thinking about them, our family and loved ones. It is difficult if not impossible to explain what it is like until you have been there and gone through it. Like I said it was pretty sad, and AFRTS (Armed Forces Radio Television Services) kept playing Christmas songs, and Elvis Presley singing Blue Christmas played way too many time to suit my needs even though it was very appropriate and suited the occasion.

The day passed as rapidly as the rest, but the night would come and all thoughts of family and friends had to be stuffed back in the recesses of our minds where they would not come and make us weak or cause us to loose concentration on where we were and what our mission was. Night time always seemed like it lasted an eternity, and in some cases there was the probability that it would be, maybe in many cases, you never really knew, all you knew was you were here now, and this too would pass, just as everything else would. It was just a matter of where you would be when the morning sun came up, or if you would be at all. Each and every situation is temporary and that meant life, as we know it in the here and now is only temporal; we begin to die the day we are born. The only guarantee is we will not get out of here alive if the enemy has anything to say about it, and that is the only absolute guarantee we have. Our mission is to defeat this guarantee, and finish our tour so we can get home to whatever awaits us. We are heroes and outlaws and sometimes they are the same, we try to do right but to some it is a game. The law of the states is designed for the rich and the blood that we shed means nothing to cops and the Judge. Lawyers are hypocrites and liars for pay and the only hope we have is enough to pay to get a good mouthpiece. No matter the crime you can always walk free if you have enough money to pay the right fee. Everything has a price, it only matters how much you are willing or capable of paying.

We raise our children on lies and have convinced ourselves they are harmless and good for their growth, it helps them to develop their imagination and creativity. We teach them of Santa and Easter bunnies, goblins and ghosts and witches and all. Our children believe Santa will bring them their gifts if they have been good, after all the gifts we give are more often then we choose to accept stuck in some closet and found when someone has the task of inventorying our personal affects when we die and determine what goes to whom. So we impatiently await a man in red suit. We slip in the gifts and forget what the season is about, we are not Wise men and they are not Christ, so why the gifts? We as Christians have already received our gifts, we have eternal life because of the sacrifice of Jesus Christ and now for our freedom we too must sacrifice and fight a war we know little about. We are taught not to kill and yet when the government tells us it is a necessary evil it becomes okay and we are even rewarded for it. Now killing is right, we must protect the freedom of those unjustly forced to endure communist rule, we are the Crusaders of Justice and all that is right yet we do the same thing as the enemy does only we justify it with a philosophy and doctrine, a promise of freedom for all the oppressed, wrong becomes right and the accomplishment of the mission is all that counts. The more we kill the better, this is what we are told would end the war sooner. The sooner we end the war the less will have to lose their lives and the lives of their loved ones. Somehow this seems like an oxymoron. Then who am I a common Marine to question; after all they have complete groups of people to study these things, appointed by the Executive Office of the United States.

In the meantime I will walk in the valley of the shadow of death and I will fear no evil as I am the baddest and meanest Mother in the valley, I will fear not the enemy for my rifle and ammo will comfort me and my enemy will fall down before me as I am the bearer of the banner of justice.

So Merry Christmas to all and good cheer to you too from our place of duty in the armpit of humanity, VIETNAM, Laos, Cambodia, or where ever the hell we really are!

The Unknown Truth

The truth will never be known by most of mainstream society and for those of us who do know it will never be able to completely relay the entire truth as we know it. To know the real truth you would have to have been there at the time and place we were there.

The whole experience was too horrific for us to relay to those we love. We do not what those we love to have to deal with or ever experience such atrocities themselves. We are protectors, and we will burden the weight of the nasty truth. Only we can since we are the only ones who have seen it as it was and through our eyes. Eyes wide open and void of the innocence we have lost through this experience of futility. A world without compassion, love, concern or even humane consideration for a people we were sent to protect and serve.

Eyes wide open forever more! In war we are reduced to the lowest form of existence and in that situation atrocities occur and the innocent get hurt, although sad, it is a fact of life, a reality of war. Maybe we should tell the truth, the whole ugly truth so people will know what war is like and just maybe by the grace of God be a bit more hesitant about jumping into another one. But then it is not the people that generate and send troops to war it is the governments and to them we are just pieces of meat to feed the fierce lion, the ugly dragon. We are the peons and it means little to nothing to send us to war as the folks in the government have forgotten how it are to be working class people, we Veteran's have simply and heartlessly become a number. They have become complacent about us and high-minded about themselves. Mostly narcissistic and they are important they are all we should care about in their minds, they have become above the law and free of the worry of them and theirs being carted off to some obscure combat zone. We are only the people, subservient to them. Additionally it is the perpetrator that suffers in the end as he strives to cross back over to the moral normality of mainstream society and gets smacked by the mainstream, as we are now crazy drug addicts and alcoholics. When our country needed us and placed the call, we answered

When we look at our children as they are growing up we can not help but think of all we have seen and done, and just pray our children are never forced to endure this type of existence and pain and suffering as well as that we had forced on others as we were forced to inflict by being forced to be here and accomplish whatever good we were suppose to be accomplishing. I guess the question is in all of our minds, are the South Vietnamese better off that we were there then before we went?

About Our Veteran

In all probability I should have addressed this issue in the beginning of the book but it dawned on me that many may not even know the truth of who, what and where the combat veteran actually come from. Let me introduce him or in today's times, her, at this juncture. He is a father/Mother, a son/daughter, a brother/sister, a cousin or uncle/aunt. He may be a boyfriend/girlfriend, fiancé, or husband/wife. They may be your Pastor at Church, a Deacon, the store cashier, the one that carried your groceries out to your car for a tip. They could be the local car salesperson, the cable person or the telephone repairperson. They could have been a local cop or fireman. They could have been part of or at the very least touched every facet of your life. Some were the high school football players or cheerleaders. Others like Private Numbnuts could have been one of the trouble- makers on the local street corner. They grew up in good home; foster homes and some were wards of the state and considered incorrigible and in Juvenile Detention. Just maybe that someone was you! Maybe you are one like me that part of you died so many years ago in some far off obscure place where you can not even remember the cities and places you were, only the particular sounding name of some strange place with strange philosophies and ways.

215

The average age of the military man is 19 years going on 100 at times and 12 at other times. He/she is a short haired, tight-muscled kid who, under normal circumstances is considered by society as half man, half boy almost women yet still a girl. Not yet dry behind the ears, not old enough to buy a beer, but old enough to die for his or her country. They probably started to work as young kids earning their own money by age eleven or twelve doing odd jobs. They would rather wax their own car that they had worked and earned the money to pay for than wash the family vehicle. He or she is a recent High School drop-out with a GED, High School Graduate or local Community College graduate, and in rare cases a college graduate; he was probably a below average or average student, pursued some form of sport activities, or musical instrument. He/she drives a ten- year -old jalopy, and has a steady girlfriend/boyfriend that either broke up with him when he left, after he/she left because they could not bare the thought of loosing someone close to them, or swears to be waiting when he/she returns from half a world away. He listens to rock and roll or hip-hop or rap or jazz or swing or Country, and a 155mm howitzer.

He/she is 10 or 15 pounds lighter now than when he/she was at home because he/she is working or fighting from before dawn to well after dusk. He/she has trouble spelling, thus letter writing is a pain for him/her, but he/she can field strip a rifle in 30 seconds and reassemble it in less time in the dark. He/She can recite to you the nomenclature of a machine gun or grenade launcher and use either one effectively if he/she must. He/she digs foxholes and latrines and can apply first aid like a professional. He/she can march until he/she is told to stop, or stop until they are told to march. They obey orders instantly and without hesitation, but he/she is not without spirit or individual dignity. He/she is self-sufficient. They have two sets of fatigues: they wash one and wear the other. They have learned to keep their canteens full and their feet dry. They may in their hectic lives forget to brush their teeth, but never to clean their rifle. They can cook their own meals even when they must often get very creative. They can mend their own clothes, and fix their own hurts. If you're thirsty, they'll share their water with you; if you are hungry, their food. They'll even split their ammunition with you in the midst of battle when you run low. He/she has learned to use his/her hands like weapons and weapons like they were his/her hands. He/she can save your life - or take it, because that is their job. He/she will often do twice the work of a civilian, draw half the pay, and still find ironic humor in it all. They have seen more suffering and death than they should have in his/her short lifetime. He/she has wept in public and in private, for friends who have fallen in combat and is unashamed. They feel every note of the National Anthem vibrate through their body while at rigid attention, while tempering the burning desire to 'square-away ' those around them who haven't bothered to stand, remove their hat, or even stop talking. In an odd twist, day in and day out, far from home, they defend their right to be disrespectful just as did their Father, Grandfather, and Great-grandfather, he/she is paying the price for our freedom. Beardless or not, he is not a boy. They are the American Fighting Man and women that has kept this country free for over 200 years.

While We Were Away!

While we were in the battlefields of Vietnam, Laos, and Cambodia with troops and Planes in Thailand things were radically changing at home. There were riots and demonstrations in cities and towns of hometown USA and on the college campuses. Everyone professed to be a voice for the downtrodden, uneducated and mislead but the truth is they had their own agendas and were misleading those young pal able minds that were entering college and the work force. Most were cowards seeking draft deferments. They preached Peace and love then threw rocks and attacked people who had different opinions, this showed their true colors. The quasi-Pentecostal Charismatic Evangelical Ministry had taken hold and every Sunday morning they would preach to the multitudes and people were confused and through fast talking Charismatic's they would send the money to be prayed for and for this evil country to be prayed for as they would preach we were in the end times and needed to make personal changes immediately.

The President was caught lying to the people and even though this was nothing new and it had existed long before now, it had become public information so the people began to distrust the government. The music had radically changed

218

and mostly was protest and antiestablishment. Motorcycle clubs were growing strong and commanding larger numbers, contrary to popular belief, many were Vietnam Veterans fed up with our mainstream society, government, and disenchanted with the Vietnam War. Many had served their country proudly and were subjected to abuse both physically and psychologically as if the war itself had not been enough, our own citizens we thought we had went to fight for had now turned on us. We were unable to secure jobs as we were tainted and damaged goods, many of us with disabilities. Our dream of the little three- bedroom house with the white picket fence and the 9-5 job with a nice car or station wagon and two or three kids was gone. Many went off to college to get the benefits we earned, but sadly enough most would never complete college, our minds were screwed up and this was more then we could handle, besides college was about indoctrination in the new society, the one we missed out on as we were away fighting and had little to do with education. It was more about partying and using every kind of imaginable drug that we had never heard of. We had been reprogrammed from the programming we had been given from infancy until we entered the military to be warriors after entering the military and never deprogrammed so they formulated a co-society where they could be what and who they were trained to be with brothers of the same mind set, and now the government would like to eradicate them, the very people they trained. There was the Hippie movement, a good concept, make love not war, free sex, communes, each working for the good of the whole, what a beautiful philosophy. Sadly enough, we have greed, jealousy and corruption. Whenever you get too many people in one place, some will rebel and lead others astray, they will convince them they are getting less then they deserve and before you know it your group separates and what was good now dies a horrible death. It never fails, people that start out with good ideas will ultimately become corrupt with power and position and then they begin to take advantage of the others because they can. The concept is good the possibility of it working very slight if at all. It was as though the world was falling apart and no one knew which direction to go in. It seemed to be anti-everything. Everyone it appeared had his or her own agenda or ideology, it was as though Pandora's box had been opened and everyone was running in their own direction. There was the Black Panthers and their radical behaviorisms, they claimed they had been taken captive as slaves and were still oppressed. I know I personally had nothing to do with that and I had served with Blacks in Vietnam and we never had a problem. In my world we appreciated everyone in our team and unit since our lives depended on it. it took two to carry him, and besides you just may need each others blood. I heard stories of racial tensions in the military, but I guess I was fortunate as I was in small elite units and never really experienced it. The American Nazi Party, another sick bunch of personal agenda seekers professing to stand for some righteous cause. Hell, I thought we were fighting against communism and dictatorships, and yet there are those that choose to elect this type of leadership and attitude. White supremacists, which I believe fear people who are different and therefore choose to see them as inferior or other then human, well, we all bleed red and we all have feelings, we are all equal and have the same rights. Sure some of us start out with a fixed deck against us and have to try harder, but so do white trash as I was referred to because my Daddy was working class poor and would never own anything or become great according to mainstream societies standards. Everyone should have stood up for equality for all. This is what the Hippies were trying to do they just went about it the wrong way and in blind faith. Then came the problem with addiction and use of hallucinogenics, this brought the establishment down on them as well as altering the thought process. Everything was moving at mach speed but was going in no definite direction.

The only news we got was the Stars and Stripes, and that was a military paper full of its opinionated news supporting the government viewpoint and not even that of the military folks actually serving in Vietnam. Then there were reports from home and what was going on, but the reports were generally territorial in nature and fairly limited to the small area it actually originated from. We all knew things would never be the same as they were, not for us, not even for America.

I guess I was among the fortunate ones, I was in an elite unit and we really had no problems with race, religion or place of birth. We could see some philosophical and racial difficulties in some of the bigger units, but nothing in ours except the next operation or mission. Our dreams were when we would rotate back to the world (states), and what we planned on doing; little did we know how much we had changed. When we got home many of us would find we were square pegs trying to fit in round holes, and that is how much of the rest of our life would be. For us, the real combat soldier, we would become heads (drug abusers); there was a multitude of drugs, Psychedelic like LSD, opiates, and THC. The enemy was very smart and introduced drugs to the American service members as a form of psychological warfare and many would become addicted to them by trying to escape the pain of emotions and feelings, rendering them pretty much non-productive members of society. Then we had the juicers, (Alcohol abusers) and some of us would use both, a definite cocktail to meet with the Grim Reaper, both to try to escape anxiety attacks, panic attacks, constant flashbacks, and to just get some small amount of sleep without the severe nightmares associated with death and dying, being chased and falling. These nightmares always led to the knowledge that if whatever it was that was chasing you ever caught you or if you finally hit bottom while falling it was over for you and you would die which to most of us was not so bad if we did not have to suffer the nightmares first. Many would commit suicide as a means to escape or find peace of mind, many more would attempt suicide and live to regret not succeeding, some would later be glad they had failed. All would have scars that in most cases were not visible, but ever present.

We were called baby-killers, spit on and ridiculed for doing what we were taught was right. Now here we were sacrificing ourselves for a cause we believed in and now we were put down and talked about as though we were a bunch of mercenaries! Worse yet many of us doubted who we were and why we were told to do what we were and what we had accomplished, especially since we left Vietnam never being allowed to complete our mission. We could have won the war several times if the Politicians would have stayed out of it and allowed us to fight the war as a war. Instead they wanted to tie one hand behind us and send in the news media and their sensationalism. Most reporters wrote what would make them look good, give them notoriety so they could secure employment and better pay while the foot soldier they damaged in doing so would suffer from it for all time as would his family.

If I were to say anything good came of the Vietnam War, it would be that it was an awakening time for the American people and what was going on within the government. People began to learn that democracy and freedom were not exactly the same; we are free as long as we comply with government constraints and dictates federal, state, county, city and sometimes neighborhood. You can own your own place as long as you pay your taxes, you can build what you want as long as you comply with zoning standards, get a permit to build, and pay the taxes on it. Our legal system is directly commensurate to your bank account. The poor man is guilty until proven innocent.

Where things changed so radically I don't know, or did they, maybe the veil dropped and the truth was exposed for what it was, we lost our blinders, or was it us that changed and became the square peg I earlier described in a world of round holes. A people too closely controlled by government and enslaved by excessive laws is a people that looses initiative and innovation and begins to die.

In Summation

There are no winners in war, everyone suffers and the innocent are the ones that get the brunt of it, collateral damage they call it. The rich get richer and the poor die young. The folks that say," You made it back, you are one of the lucky ones, you made it". What they do not know is we are lucky all right, we get to live with the atrocities and memories of what we did and seen done. Those that died in country are free from the memories and will never suffer the indignity we endured when we returned. So many of us Combat Vietnam Veterans would have been better off not making it back, this is not just an off the cuff statement, but I as a Counselor have actually had veterans tell me this is how they felt. They have nightmares and flashbacks of things from the past that they cannot get away from. Atrocities happen all the time in war it is just easier to believe we can fight a clean war.

Even though there seems to have been a change in America, we are still having a hard time adjusting. I have on numerous occasions been Thanked for my Service to our country and had folks tell me welcome home, but it was far to late for the vast amount of us, the damage had already been done, we were irreparably damaged for life. The awakening came much too late if indeed it is an awakening.

224

Now we are in another war we have no chance of winning and it is beginning to look a whole lot like another war we remember well, Vietnam!

The biggest question that haunts my mind today is are the South Vietnamese people better off now that we were there then they were before we went? Just what did we actually accomplish while we were there?

What Became Of
The Vietnam Combat Veteran?

A part of us, the combat veterans, died in Vietnam and was left behind, irretrievable. Many of us came back to failed relationships and adjustment problems. Of course many of us had adjustment or personality disorders prior to entering the military and this just aggravated it and took some over the edge. Our loved ones felt we had changed, but how much had the news media and general social opinion changed them towards us, in our minds we did not see the change as so obvious. We felt we were finally just being us without the social facades. After all we all wear different faces for different groups or specific people or positions we play. We have a face for our family, one for our job, one for our spouse and yet another for our friends. It did not take long before our loved ones turned on us and started to avoid us.

It seemed as though the world we knew no longer existed, everything had changed, or was it us that had so drastically changed, maybe a combination of both. Several of the Vietnam veterans went back to Thailand and ran guns and drugs through the Golden Triangle through Laos, Cambodia and Vietnam. They knew how to survive there, most of those died young, some got rich and live in Thailand today very well off. Many others went off to obscurity and lived in the boonies and woods of our great country the one they thought they had fought for living off the wealth of the land out of mainstream society. Then some bureaucrat hunts them down and tells them they could not trespass, as someone or some corporation owned the land. Many crawled in the bottle and some died before they ever pulled out of it. Many others turned to drugs; after all they got a head start from the prescription drugs, mostly opiate based, given them by the Veterans Administration to keep them quiet. It appeared the Veterans Administration had a philosophy that we treat with medication until we can find the best medication to allow for some quality of life, and if we could not find the best medication, they would vegetate. This way the veteran was no harm to himself or anyone else until a better medication or treatment came along. Truth is once we are vegetated we are all but forgotten, we go to the Veterans Administration Clinics and get our twenty minutes with the Doctor and have our prescriptions renewed. Several of us, like myself was married four times and now the fifth seems to be working out just fine. The divorces were not because they did not love us, it is just very difficult to live with a PTSD victim, your life is changed and every place you go is planned around the disease, like avoiding crowds, sitting with your back to the wall if you go to a restaurant. So I as with many other combat Vietnam veterans went through one relationship after another never truly allowing anyone in completely, even when in a relationship they were all alone. There is always the fear of them leaving or dying on you so you avoid that inner heart type relationship, the total commitment that is required for a healthy relationship to flourish. How often I have heard that I was one hell'uva good friend but a lousy husband. Some ended up in Mental

Health hospitals and after the government stopped the funding in the 1980's, they were on the streets and ended up in jails or prisons and several died on the streets and were buried in state cemeteries unknown. There were those that were killed in gang fights and street fights. More then any other war we have veterans in therapy and on medication for the rest of their lives. They suffer from anxiety attacks, and panic attacks with flashbacks over thirty years later.

During World War II, Korea, and even in Iraq and Afghanistan we were sent over as a unit but in Vietnam we were sent over as replacement Items, like a vehicle or weapons. Too many were victims and perpetrators of domestic violence due to uncontrollable anger issues. We live with the past and too often I hear those who say get over it and on with life, but how do you get over something that died so many years ago in a country that is no better off now then when we entered it. Sure there are many of us Vietnam Veterans who have been very successful, then there are the ones that have worked mediocre jobs never wanting to be in charge, not wanting to accept responsibility for others as we were forced to do in Vietnam.

Rest assured we all have our moments from time to time when memories come rushing back and none of us who actually served in combat in Vietnam will ever completely forget the experience no matter how hard we try or how hard we try to convince ourselves and others. For the combat Vietnam Veteran it is an experience we will take to the grave with us. When I refer to the combat Veteran, I am talking about the ones out front actually fighting, for every one Grunt we have somewhere around sixteen in the rear echelon supporting us. Not everyone who professes to be a Vietnam veteran is actually a combat Vietnam veteran.

There are also those who were rear echelon that were forced to have to go to the bush to maintain and repair equipment while under incoming fire from the enemy.

May your God, as you perceive God to be, Bless the future generations of Warriors as they leave the comforts of their homes and those that love them and they love to serve in a foreign country, and God forbid if we ever have to fight on our own lands. In the end we were ridiculed, and put down. When the war was over, it would just begin for us the veterans, as we had to fight our own government to get benefits we were promised and now we have to fight to keep our benefits, we believed were inherit, we were in many cases shuffled off to obscure hospitals and for got about. We also had to fight our own countryman to have peace and be able to live among those with limited knowledge and understanding of what we had undergone. Then when the nightmares began we were treated with medication, and if the correct drug was not found we were vegetated with things like lithium and Prozac. Then in the eighties the federal government quit funding the mental hospitals, and we were thrown in the streets many on heavy sedatives and opiates. We were cut off and then the prisons began to fill up from crimes committed to get the necessary fix the medication use to give us. We found we no longer fit into mainstream society, we became known as sociological misfits. This is why I am forced to list this book as fiction, but we the Grunts know the truth! Wars are not fought being nice, fair, civil or for that matter even humane. Even though we signed the Geneva Convention which supposedly established a set or rules of do's and do not's it was not even worth the paper it was written on. Wars create or generate it's own rules at the very moment in which you must make a decision or perform an action. Predetermined rules cause the person or persons who abide by them to be the weaker of the warriors and more often then not the one who gives his or her life for a cause. If not the epitome of oxymoron's is the statement and worse yet the belief that there is or ever could be a clean fight. That type of thought comes from the protected and inexperienced.

When we fight against a formidable enemy we need to introduce the shock factor, we need to strike fear in the enemy anyway we can possibly do it. In Vietnam they believed they would go to their eternal peace if they died fighting for the cause and then only if they were in tact, had all their body parts, legs, arms and so on. If you wanted to induce fear into them you had to dismember and decapitate the enemy. The South Koreans figured this out right away, for the most part, Asians are true warriors and when they fight an enemy they mean to win no matter what it takes. We Europeans believe there is a thing as clean fighting, at least those who have never been forced to be in the pits actually doing the fighting. Somehow mainstream society still expects us to fight a clean war being humane. They actually have certain weapons we can use and those we are not suppose to. When you are in the pits you use everything in your arsenal to defeat but also instill total fear in the enemy, if you can instill enough fear you can defeat the enemy psychologically destroying his will to fight. You can for damn sure bet the enemy will do everything possible to destroy our will to fight and they will kill and dismember and bring shame to us even in our death and they need not worry about some idiotic news media sensationalizing the news story to sell papers. You can bet your sweet ass they are not and need not worry about getting a Court-martial for actions in combat. They are not judged on how they fight the war only if they win or loose. America needs to let it's warriors fight to win and accept the reality war is hell and there is nothing clean about it.

Now we have a new war and a new set of veterans who are suffering, and they now take precedence over the Vietnam Veteran. I can only hope and pray we are not soon forgotten and shoved on the back burner. A country that forgets it's veterans of past wars soon losses its freedom. What would we expect when holidays like Memorial day become nothing but a long weekend and a good time for a drunk with time to sober up and get well for work on the Tuesday we went back to work. Then when you really think about it we live in a time of diminishing freedom with more government controls then ever in recorded history of free America. Peoples will freely give up rights and freedoms when they are in fear, then one day they wake up but it is too late, they have given the Governments all the controls, too much power over the people with not enough controls on the government itself.

ΔΔΔΔΔ

CPSIA information can be obtained at www.ICGtesting.com
Printed in the USA

245506LV00001B/216/P